The Success Journal: Limited Edition

ISBN: 979-8-9853082-3-5

© Copyright 2021 Stacia Pierce Ultimate Lifestyle Enterprises, LLC
All Rights Reserved

Reproduction or translation of any part of this work is unlawful. No part of this document may be reproduced or transmitted in any form or by any means, electronic, mechanical, photocopying, recording, or otherwise, without prior written permission of Stacia Pierce/Ultimate Lifestyle Enterprises LLC.

This product is designed to provide authoritative information in regard to the subject matter covered. It is sold with the understanding that the publisher is not engaged in rendering nor is responsible for, legal, or accounting services. If legal, accounting or industry specific advice is required, the services of a competent professional in those areas should be sought.

The Success Journal

This Journal Belongs to:

_____

Month of:

_____

MY WORD
for the month

[   ]

Write one word that will become your core intention to accomplish or focus on this month.

As an avid collector of journals, I've learned to harness the power of the written word to shape my life into what it is today. You can literally write your way to success when you get alone with your dreams, a great pen and an awesome journal (like this one). Consider the blank pages of a journal as the canvas of your life. What's written can soon become real for you. I encourage you to be bold enough to record your wildest dreams, greatest desires and big vision right on these pages.

The Success Journal is filled with personal prompts to conjure up amazing ideas so that you can fill the pages of this book with inspirational affirmations, aspirations and anecdotes that will keep you motivated to pursue your wildest dreams.

It is designed as a monthly journal to keep your thoughts organized. You can quickly label the month and just for one month keep all of your thoughts recorded into one space. This is one of my biggest success secrets. I've been writing and organizing my thoughts in journals this way for over 20 years. This is the easiest and most effective way to retrieve information when you need it most. Sound fun right? Trust me…it really is!

This journal is also organized by weeks so that you can categorize your information on a weekly basis and start the process all over again seven days later. At the back of this journal you'll find a bonus section featuring over 30 manifestation pages for this special **Success Journal: Limited Edition**.

When you're done filling up your journal, you'll truly have a work of art—a powerful illustration of everything that is important to you. This is how you live intentionally. It's a process of identifying your wants and needs, crystalizing it on paper and then taking action to bring it to life.

Start your day with your Success Journal by writing your top three daily goals and end your day by writing what you're grateful for…these tiny actions can turn an average existence into an extraordinary adventure.
It's time you lived your best life!

Empowering you to succeed,
Dr. Stacia Pierce

How to Use the Success Journal

1. My Enjoy Life Plans

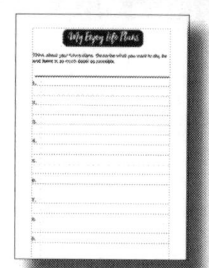

List your future plans. What do you want to do, be and have in life? There is only one copy of this page.

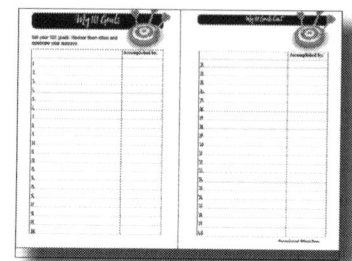

2. 101 Goals

Write your goals for this year. List your dreams and desires.

3. Write Your Life's Story

Use this page to write your story, where do you see yourself in the near future? Choose a word to focus on for this month. There is only one of these.

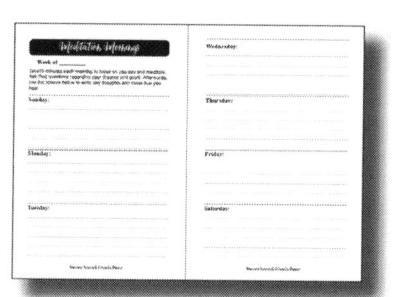

4. Meditation Mornings

I am a strong believer in meditation. Take 15 minutes daily to focus on yourself and ask God questions. These pages appear multiple times so there is enough for each week in the month.

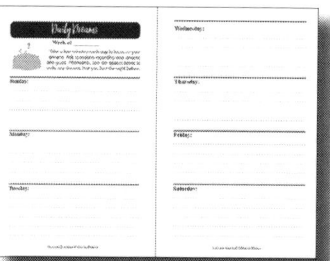

5. Daily Dreams

I am a vivid dreamer. Before bed, ask God questions. When you arise, write the answers and ideas that were revealed in your dreams.

6 My List

After your daily morning meditation, write down your weekly list. This page is repeated weekly.

7 The Big I am

How do you see yourself? Finish the sentence, I am...

8 Quotes AND Affirmations

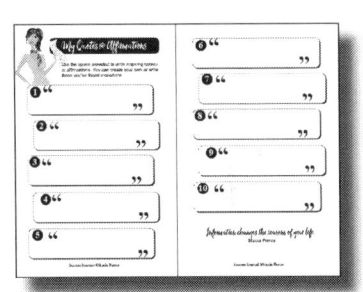

Use the 10 spaces to jot down quotes you've heard recently that inspire you or write your own.

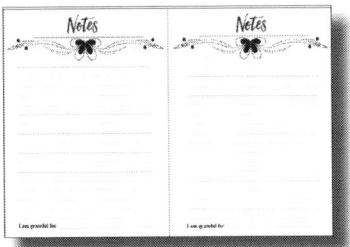

9 Notes

There are several copies of these pages per section, be sure to write your thoughts and what you're grateful for each day.

10 Book Notes

Use this space to write about the latest book you're reading and include any aha's or memorable details.

11 Manifest Your Money AND My Intentional Deposit

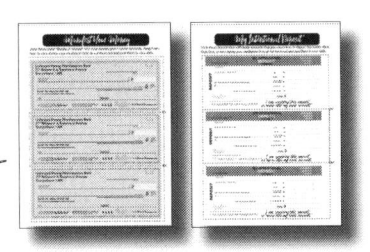

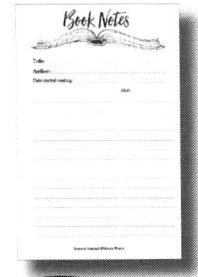

There are checks and deposit slips for you to fill out with your desired money manifestation amount as a visualization tool.

Bonus Section

My Manifestation List — 12

List what you desire to manifest.

My Luxurious Life — 13

List the items and activities that make you feel luxurious.

My Best Life Script — 14

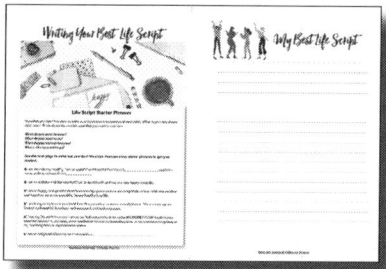

Write about who you want to become and the life you want to create. Get emotionally connected as if it's already done.

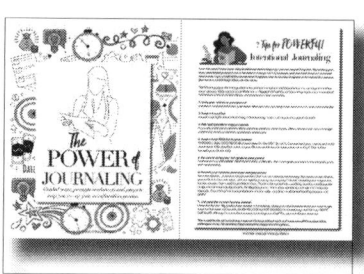

The Power of Wealth Journaling — 15

Write your way out of money challenges with my go-to process to manifest wealth.

My Money Tracker — 16

Be grateful as you generate increase, track the sources that all your profits came in from.

17 Manifestation Affirmation

Use this two part affirmation to manifest increase into your life.

18 Manifestation Worksheets & Props

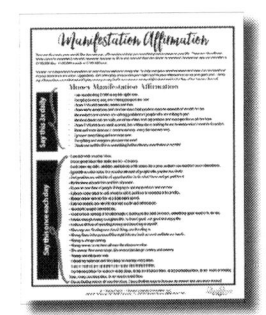

Use these manifestation worksheets and props to dream, plan and manifest your desires in all areas of your life.

My Enjoy Life Plans

Think about your future plans. Describe what you want to **do, be** and *have* in as much detail as possible.

1. _____

2. _____

3. _____

4. _____

5. _____

6. _____

7. _____

8. _____

9. _____

My Enjoy Life Plans Continued

10.

11.

12.

13.

14.

15.

16.

17.

18.

19.

20.

My 101 Goals

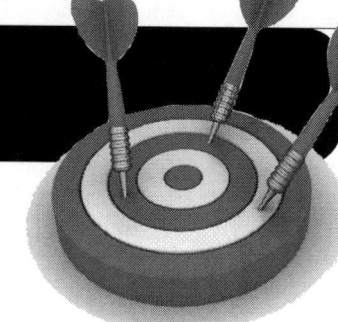

Set your 101 goals. Review them often and celebrate your success.

	Accomplished by:
1.	
2.	
3.	
4.	
5.	
6.	
7.	
8.	
9.	
10.	
11.	
12.	
13.	
14.	
15.	
16.	
17.	
18.	
19.	
20.	

Success Journal ©Stacia Pierce

My 101 Goals Cont

	Accomplished by:
21.	
22.	
23.	
24.	
25.	
26.	
27.	
28.	
29.	
30.	
31.	
32.	
33.	
34.	
35.	
36.	
37.	
38.	
39.	
40.	

Success Journal ©Stacia Pierce

My 101 Goals Cont

	Accomplished by:
41.	
42.	
43.	
44.	
45.	
46.	
47.	
48.	
49.	
50.	
51.	
52.	
53.	
54.	
55.	
56.	
57.	
58.	
59.	
60.	

Success Journal ©Stacia Pierce

My 101 Goals Cont

	Accomplished by:
61.	
62.	
63.	
64.	
65.	
66.	
67.	
68.	
69.	
70.	
71.	
72.	
73.	
74.	
75.	
76.	
77.	
78.	
79.	
80.	

My 101 Goals Cont

	Accomplished by:
81.	
82.	
83.	
84.	
85.	
86.	
87.	
88.	
89.	
90.	
91.	
92.	
93.	
94.	
95.	
96.	
97.	
98.	
99.	
100.	
101.	

Success Journal ©Stacia Pierce

Write Your Life's Success Story

Think big, dream big and write your life's story. What do you want your life's story to look like this month?

_____
_____
_____
_____
_____
_____
_____
_____
_____
_____
_____
_____
_____
_____
_____

Success Journal ©Stacia Pierce

I am Manifesting...

What do you want to manifest in your life? Write about it below.

Manifest Your Money

Write these blank checks to yourself with your current goal income amounts. Keep them here to view during your meditation time or cut them out and post them to view daily.

Unlimited Money Manifestation Bank
777 Believe it & Receive it Avenue
Everywhere, I AM

1111

DATE _____

$ _____

PAY TO THE ORDER OF _____ DOLLARS

This is a visualization tool from Dr. Stacia and Ariana Pierce

BANK OF WEALTH FOR ME
This is not an instrument subject to Article # of the UCC

FOR _____ Signed: _____

⑆00000 4444⑆ 000000 529⑈ 1111   *imagine. improve. increase.* www.lifecoach2women.com

---

Unlimited Money Manifestation Bank
777 Believe it & Receive it Avenue
Everywhere, I AM

1111

DATE _____

$ _____

PAY TO THE ORDER OF _____ DOLLARS

This is a visualization tool from Dr. Stacia and Ariana Pierce

BANK OF WEALTH FOR ME
This is not an instrument subject to Article # of the UCC

FOR _____ Signed: _____

⑆00000 4444⑆ 000000 529⑈ 1111   *imagine. improve. increase.* www.lifecoach2women.com

---

Unlimited Money Manifestation Bank
777 Believe it & Receive it Avenue
Everywhere, I AM

1111

DATE _____

$ _____

PAY TO THE ORDER OF _____ DOLLARS

This is a visualization tool from Dr. Stacia and Ariana Pierce

BANK OF WEALTH FOR ME
This is not an instrument subject to Article # of the UCC

FOR _____ Signed: _____

⑆00000 4444⑆ 000000 529⑈ 1111   *imagine. improve. increase.* www.lifecoach2women.com

My Intentional Deposit

Fill in these deposit slips with dollar amounts that you would love to deposit this month. Keep them here to view during your meditation time or cut them out and post them to view daily.

MY INTENTIONAL DEPOSIT TICKET

CHECKING ☐
SAVINGS ☐
OTHER ☐

your financial institution

Today's Date

Customer Name (Please Print)

CASH ▶
CHECK ▶
TOTAL FROM OTHER SIDE ▶
SUBTOTAL
CASH BACK ▶

Sign Here (If cash is received from this deposit)
X

▼ Start your account number here

TOTAL $

imagine. improve. increase.

Intended for visualization purposes only

⑈777000000⑈ ⑆444400000⑆

I am receiving this amount or more into my bank account.

MY INTENTIONAL DEPOSIT TICKET

CHECKING ☐
SAVINGS ☐
OTHER ☐

your financial institution

Today's Date

Customer Name (Please Print)

CASH ▶
CHECK ▶
TOTAL FROM OTHER SIDE ▶
SUBTOTAL
CASH BACK ▶

Sign Here (If cash is received from this deposit)
X

▼ Start your account number here

TOTAL $

imagine. improve. increase.

Intended for visualization purposes

⑈777000000⑈ ⑆444400000⑆

I am receiving this amount or more into my bank account.

MY INTENTIONAL DEPOSIT TICKET

CHECKING ☐
SAVINGS ☐
OTHER ☐

your financial institution

Today's Date

Customer Name (Please Print)

CASH ▶
CHECK ▶
TOTAL FROM OTHER SIDE ▶
SUBTOTAL
CASH BACK ▶

Sign Here (If cash is received from this deposit)
X

▼ Start your account number here

TOTAL $

imagine. improve. increase.

Intended for visualization purposes only

⑈777000000⑈ ⑆444400000⑆

I am receiving this amount or more into my bank account.

Book Notes

Title:

Author:

Date started reading:

Aha's

Success Journal ©Stacia Pierce

Book Notes

Title: _____

Author: _____

Date started reading: _____

                                                Aha's

Success Journal ©Stacia Pierce

You were created to thrive.

Your dream doesn't have an expiration date, so keep going for it.

The Big I am

Write a positive affirmation about where you are headed by finishing the statement:

I am...

Meditation Mornings

Week of _____

Take 15 minutes each morning to focus on your day and meditate. Ask God questions regarding your dreams and goals. Afterwards, use the spaces below to write any thoughts and ideas that you hear.

Sunday:

Monday:

Tuesday:

Success Journal ©Stacia Pierce

Wednesday:

Thursday:

Friday:

Saturday:

Success Journal ©Stacia Pierce

Daily Dreams

Week of _____

Take a few minutes each day to focus on your dreams. Ask questions regarding your dreams and goals. Afterwards, use the spaces below to write any dreams that you had the night before.

Sunday:

_____
_____
_____
_____

Monday:

_____
_____
_____
_____

Tuesday:

_____
_____
_____
_____

Success Journal ©Stacia Pierce

Wednesday:

Thursday:

Friday:

Saturday:

Success Journal ©Stacia Pierce

My List

for the week of _____

- [ ] 1.
- [ ] 2.
- [ ] 3.
- [ ] 4.
- [ ] 5.
- [ ] 6.
- [ ] 7.
- [ ] 8.
- [ ] 9.
- [ ] 10.
- [ ] 11.
- [ ] 12.
- [ ] 13.
- [ ] 14.
- [ ] 15.
- [ ] 16.

- [ ] **17.**
- [ ] **18.**
- [ ] **19.**
- [ ] **20.**
- [ ] **21.**
- [ ] **22.**
- [ ] **23.**
- [ ] **24.**
- [ ] **25.**
- [ ] **26.**
- [ ] **27.**
- [ ] **28.**
- [ ] **29.**
- [ ] **30.**
- [ ] **31.**
- [ ] **32.**
- [ ] **33.**
- [ ] **34.**
- [ ] **35.**
- [ ] **36.**

My Quotes and Affirmations

Use the space provided to write inspiring quotes or affirmations. You can create your own or write those you've found elsewhere.

1. " "

2. " "

3. " "

4. " "

5. " "

Success Journal ©Stacia Pierce

6 " "

7 " "

8 " "

9 " "

10 " "

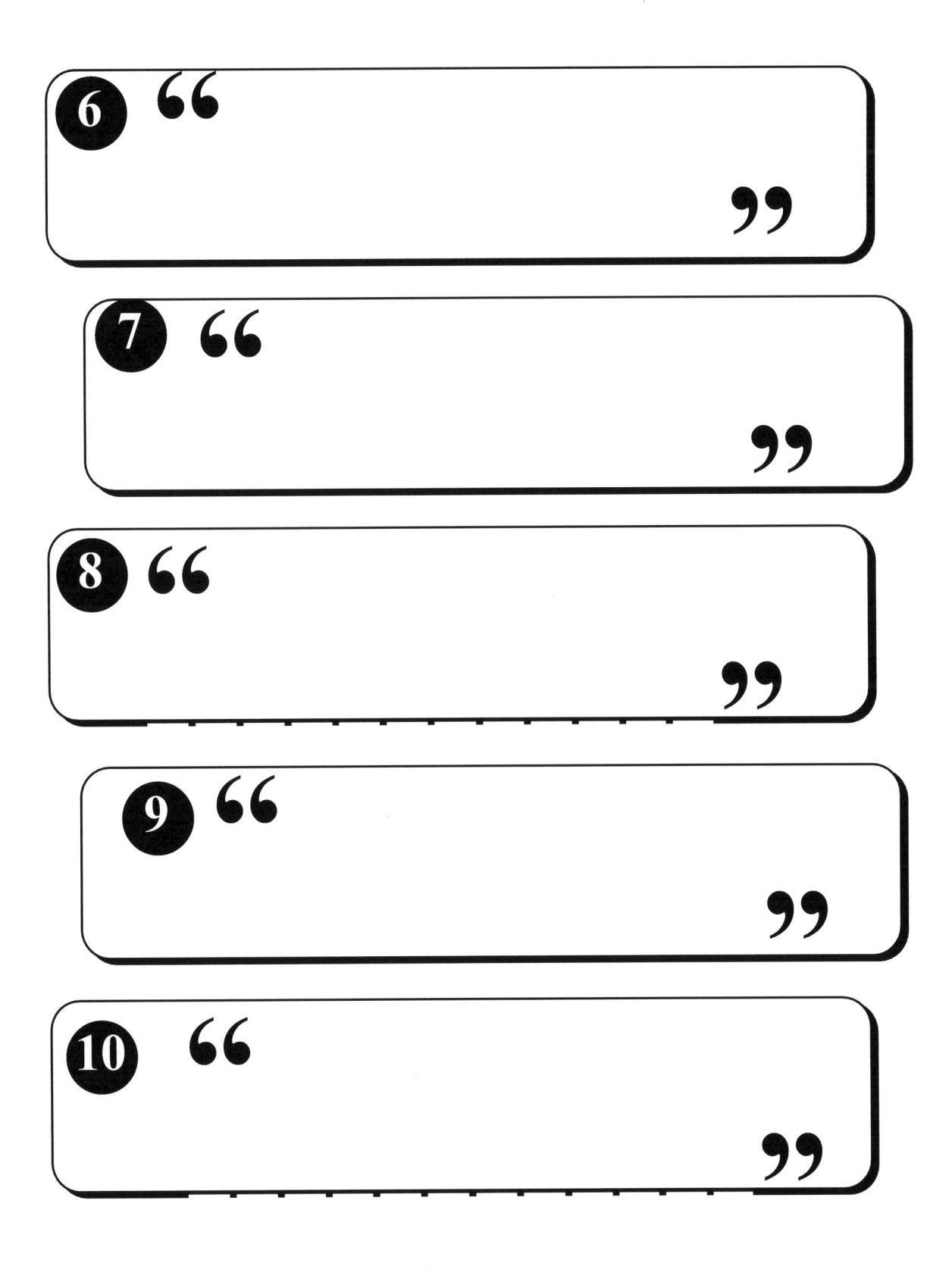

Information changes the seasons of your life.
- Stacia Pierce

Success Journal ©Stacia Pierce

My Vision Statement
What I see for me.

Write about what's next. What do you see happening this week or in the near future?

Success Journal ©Stacia Pierce

My Vision Board
What I see for me.

Bring your vision statement to life by cutting and pasting pictures and words here.

Success Journal ©Stacia Pierce

Manifest Your Money

Write these blank checks to yourself with your current goal income amounts. Keep them here to view during your meditation time or cut them out and post them to view daily.

Unlimited Money Manifestation Bank
777 Believe it & Receive it Avenue
Everywhere, I AM

1111

DATE _____

$ _____

PAY TO THE ORDER OF _____ DOLLARS

This is a visualization tool from Dr. Stacia and Ariana Pierce

BANK OF WEALTH FOR ME
This is not an instrument subject to Article # of the UCC

FOR _____ Signed: _____

⑈000004444⑈ 000000529⑈ 1111   www.lifecoach2women.com

Unlimited Money Manifestation Bank
777 Believe it & Receive it Avenue
Everywhere, I AM

1111

DATE _____

$ _____

PAY TO THE ORDER OF _____ DOLLARS

This is a visualization tool from Dr. Stacia and Ariana Pierce

BANK OF WEALTH FOR ME
This is not an instrument subject to Article # of the UCC

FOR _____ Signed: _____

⑈000004444⑈ 000000529⑈ 1111   www.lifecoach2women.com

Unlimited Money Manifestation Bank
777 Believe it & Receive it Avenue
Everywhere, I AM

1111

DATE _____

$ _____

PAY TO THE ORDER OF _____ DOLLARS

This is a visualization tool from Dr. Stacia and Ariana Pierce

BANK OF WEALTH FOR ME
This is not an instrument subject to Article # of the UCC

FOR _____ Signed: _____

⑈000004444⑈ 000000529⑈ 1111   www.lifecoach2women.com

Notes Date: _____

I am grateful for _____

Success Journal ©Stacia Pierce

Notes

Date: _____

I am grateful for _____

Success Journal ©Stacia Pierce

Notes

Date: _____

_____
_____
_____
_____
_____
_____
_____
_____
_____
_____
_____
_____
_____
_____

I am grateful for _____
_____

Success Journal ©Stacia Pierce

Notes   Date:_____

_____
_____
_____
_____
_____
_____
_____
_____
_____
_____
_____
_____
_____
_____
_____
_____

I am grateful for _____
_____

Success Journal ©Stacia Pierce

Notes

Date: _____

I am grateful for _____

Success Journal ©Stacia Pierce

Notes
Date: _____

I am grateful for _____

Success Journal ©Stacia Pierce

Notes

Date: _____

I am grateful for _____

Success Journal ©Stacia Pierce

Notes

Date: _____

I am grateful for _____

Success Journal ©Stacia Pierce

Notes
Date: _____

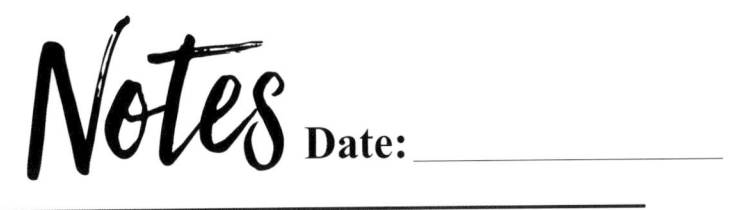

I am grateful for _____

Success Journal ©Stacia Pierce

Notes

Date: _____

I am grateful for _____

Success Journal ©Stacia Pierce

Notes

Date: _____

I am grateful for _____

Notes

Date: _____

I am grateful for _____

Success Journal ©Stacia Pierce

Notes

Date: _____

I am grateful for _____

Notes   Date: _____

I am grateful for _____

Notes
Date: _____

I am grateful for _____

Notes

Date: _____

I am grateful for _____

Success Journal ©Stacia Pierce

Notes
Date: _____

I am grateful for _____

Notes

Date: _____

I am grateful for _____

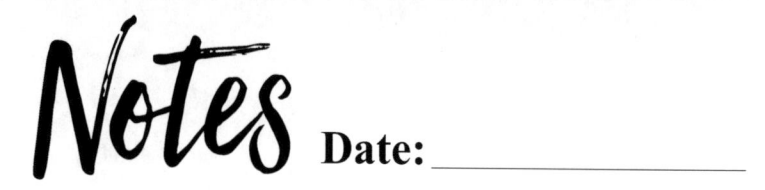

Success Journal ©Stacia Pierce

Notes
Date: _____

I am grateful for _____

Success Journal ©Stacia Pierce

Notes
Date: _____

I am grateful for _____

Notes Date:_____

I am grateful for _____

Success Journal ©Stacia Pierce

Notes

Date: _____

_____
_____
_____
_____
_____
_____
_____
_____
_____
_____
_____
_____
_____
_____
_____

I am grateful for _____
_____

Success Journal ©Stacia Pierce

Notes
Date: _____

I am grateful for _____

Success Journal ©Stacia Pierce

Notes

Date:_____

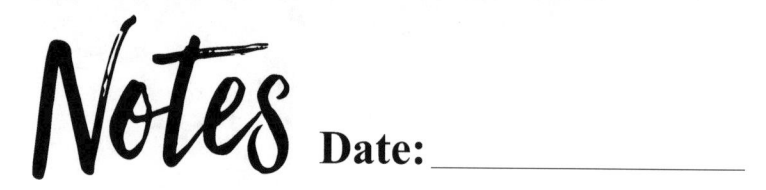

I am grateful for _____

Notes
Date: _____

I am grateful for _____

Notes

Date: _____

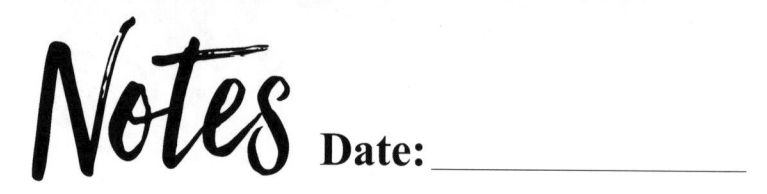

I am grateful for _____

Notes

Date: _____

_____
_____
_____
_____
_____
_____
_____
_____
_____
_____
_____
_____
_____
_____
_____

I am grateful for _____
_____

Success Journal ©Stacia Pierce

Notes

Date: _____

I am grateful for _____

Success Journal ©Stacia Pierce

Notes

Date: _____

_____
_____
_____
_____
_____
_____
_____
_____
_____
_____
_____
_____
_____
_____
_____

I am grateful for _____
_____

Success Journal ©Stacia Pierce

Notes

Date: _____

I am grateful for _____

Success Journal ©Stacia Pierce

Notes

Date: _____

I am grateful for _____

Success Journal ©Stacia Pierce

Notes

Date:_____

I am grateful for _____

Success Journal ©Stacia Pierce

If you want something BIG to happen, Expect something BIG to happen.

Success Journal ©Stacia Pierce

Stop waiting until you're perfectly ready, just start.

The Big I am

Write a positive affirmation about where you are headed by finishing the statement:

I am...

Success Journal ©Stacia Pierce

Meditation Mornings

Week of _____

Take 15 minutes each morning to focus on your day and meditate. Ask God questions regarding your dreams and goals. Afterwards, use the spaces below to write any thoughts and ideas that you hear.

Sunday:

_____
_____
_____
_____

Monday:

_____
_____
_____
_____

Tuesday:

_____
_____
_____
_____

Wednesday:

Thursday:

Friday:

Saturday:

Success Journal ©Stacia Pierce

Daily Dreams

Week of _____

Take a few minutes each day to focus on your dreams. Ask questions regarding your dreams and goals. Afterwards, use the spaces below to write any dreams that you had the night before.

Sunday:

_____
_____
_____
_____

Monday:

_____
_____
_____
_____

Tuesday:

_____
_____
_____
_____

Success Journal ©Stacia Pierce

Wednesday:

Thursday:

Friday:

Saturday:

Success Journal ©Stacia Pierce

My List

for the week of _____

- [ ] 1.
- [ ] 2.
- [ ] 3.
- [ ] 4.
- [ ] 5.
- [ ] 6.
- [ ] 7.
- [ ] 8.
- [ ] 9.
- [ ] 10.
- [ ] 11.
- [ ] 12.
- [ ] 13.
- [ ] 14.
- [ ] 15.
- [ ] 16.

- [ ] 17.
- [ ] 18.
- [ ] 19.
- [ ] 20.
- [ ] 21.
- [ ] 22.
- [ ] 23.
- [ ] 24.
- [ ] 25.
- [ ] 26.
- [ ] 27.
- [ ] 28.
- [ ] 29.
- [ ] 30.
- [ ] 31.
- [ ] 32.
- [ ] 33.
- [ ] 34.
- [ ] 35.
- [ ] 36.

Success Journal ©Stacia Pierce

My Quotes and Affirmations

Use the space provided to write inspiring quotes or affirmations. You can create your own or write those you've found elsewhere.

1. " "

2. " "

3. " "

4. " "

5. " "

Success Journal ©Stacia Pierce

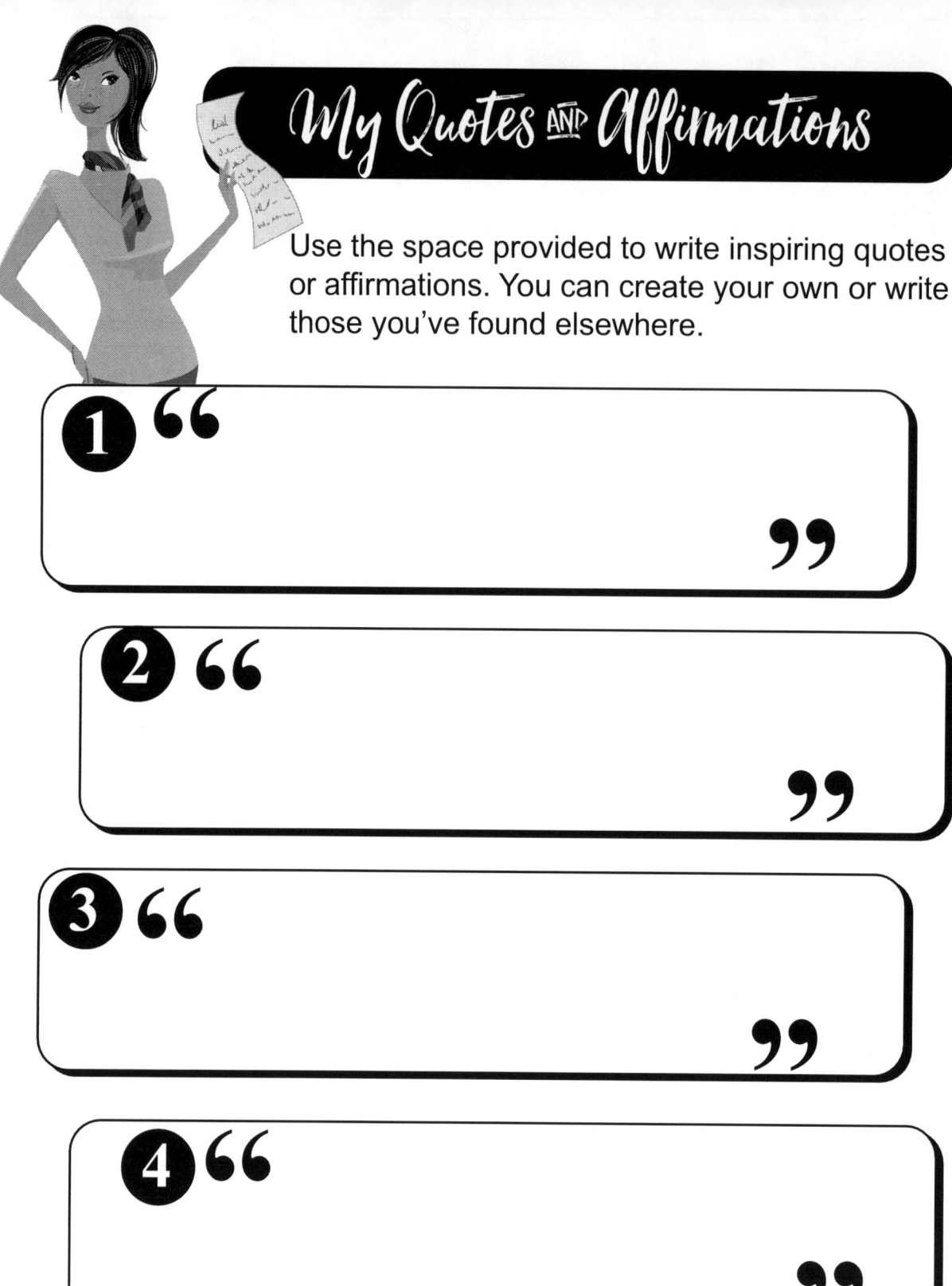

6 " "

7 " "

8 " "

9 " "

10 " "

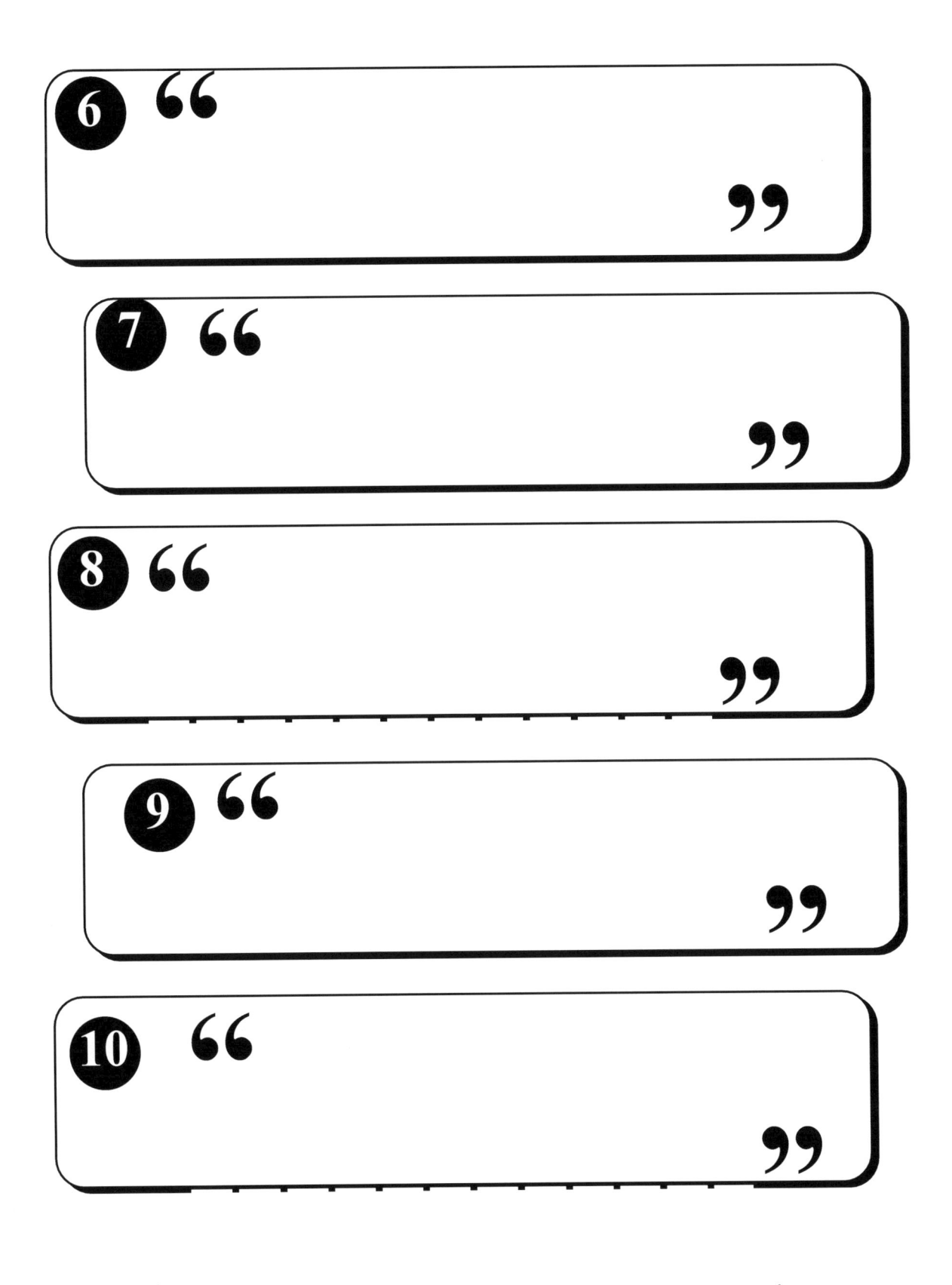

Information changes the seasons of your life.
- Stacia Pierce

My Vision Statement
What I see for me.

Write about what's next. What do you see happening this week or in the near future?

Success Journal ©Stacia Pierce

My Vision Board
What I see for me.

Bring your vision statement to life by cutting and pasting pictures and words here.

Success Journal ©Stacia Pierce

Manifest Your Money

Write these blank checks to yourself with your current goal income amounts. Keep them here to view during your meditation time or cut them out and post them to view daily.

Unlimited Money Manifestation Bank
777 Believe it & Receive it Avenue
Everywhere, I AM

No. 1111

DATE _____

$ _____

PAY TO THE ORDER OF _____

_____ DOLLARS

BANK OF WEALTH FOR ME
This is not an instrument subject to Article # of the UCC

This is a visualization tool from Dr. Stacia and Ariana Pierce

FOR _____   Signed: _____

⑂00000 4444⑂ 000000529⑈ 1111

www.lifecoach2women.com

Unlimited Money Manifestation Bank
777 Believe it & Receive it Avenue
Everywhere, I AM

No. 1111

DATE _____

$ _____

PAY TO THE ORDER OF _____

_____ DOLLARS

BANK OF WEALTH FOR ME
This is not an instrument subject to Article # of the UCC

This is a visualization tool from Dr. Stacia and Ariana Pierce

FOR _____   Signed: _____

⑂00000 4444⑂ 000000529⑈ 1111

www.lifecoach2women.com

Unlimited Money Manifestation Bank
777 Believe it & Receive it Avenue
Everywhere, I AM

No. 1111

DATE _____

$ _____

PAY TO THE ORDER OF _____

_____ DOLLARS

BANK OF WEALTH FOR ME
This is not an instrument subject to Article # of the UCC

This is a visualization tool from Dr. Stacia and Ariana Pierce

FOR _____   Signed: _____

⑂00000 4444⑂ 000000529⑈ 1111

www.lifecoach2women.com

Notes

Date: _____

I am grateful for _____

Success Journal ©Stacia Pierce

Notes

Date: _____

I am grateful for _____

Success Journal ©Stacia Pierce

Notes   Date: _____

_____
_____
_____
_____
_____
_____
_____
_____
_____
_____
_____
_____
_____
_____
_____
_____
_____
_____
_____

I am grateful for _____

Success Journal ©Stacia Pierce

Notes
Date: _____

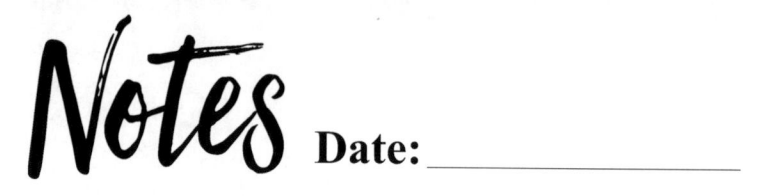

I am grateful for _____

Notes
Date: _____

I am grateful for _____

Notes

Date: _____

_____
_____
_____
_____
_____
_____
_____
_____
_____
_____
_____
_____
_____
_____
_____
_____
_____

I am grateful for _____
_____

Success Journal ©Stacia Pierce

Notes Date: _____

I am grateful for _____

Success Journal ©Stacia Pierce

Notes

Date: _____

I am grateful for _____

Success Journal ©Stacia Pierce

Notes
Date: _____

I am grateful for _____

Success Journal ©Stacia Pierce

Notes

Date: _____

I am grateful for _____

Success Journal ©Stacia Pierce

Notes
Date: _____

I am grateful for _____

Success Journal ©Stacia Pierce

Notes

Date: _____

I am grateful for _____

Success Journal ©Stacia Pierce

Notes
Date: _____

I am grateful for _____

Success Journal ©Stacia Pierce

Notes

Date: _____

I am grateful for _____

Success Journal ©Stacia Pierce

Notes

Date: _____

_____
_____
_____
_____
_____
_____
_____
_____
_____
_____
_____
_____
_____
_____
_____
_____
_____

I am grateful for _____

_____

Success Journal ©Stacia Pierce

Notes

Date: _____

I am grateful for _____

Success Journal ©Stacia Pierce

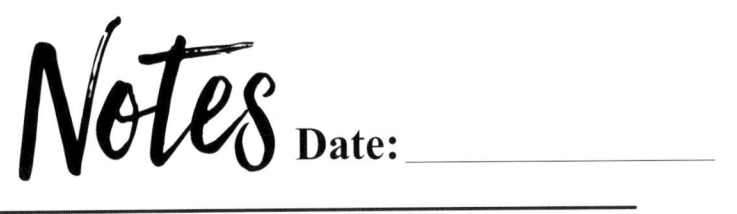

Notes
Date: _____

I am grateful for _____

Success Journal ©Stacia Pierce

Notes

Date: _____

I am grateful for _____

Success Journal ©Stacia Pierce

Notes
Date: _____

I am grateful for _____

Success Journal ©Stacia Pierce

Notes

Date: _____

I am grateful for _____

Success Journal ©Stacia Pierce

Notes
Date: _____

I am grateful for _____

Success Journal ©Stacia Pierce

Notes

Date: _____

I am grateful for _____

Success Journal ©Stacia Pierce

Notes
Date: _____

I am grateful for _____

Notes

Date: _____

I am grateful for _____

Success Journal ©Stacia Pierce

Notes
Date: _____

_____
_____
_____
_____
_____
_____
_____
_____
_____
_____
_____
_____
_____
_____
_____
_____

I am grateful for _____
_____

Success Journal ©Stacia Pierce

Notes
Date: _____

I am grateful for _____

Success Journal ©Stacia Pierce

Notes

Date: _____

_____
_____
_____
_____
_____
_____
_____
_____
_____
_____
_____
_____
_____
_____
_____

I am grateful for _____

_____

Success Journal ©Stacia Pierce

Notes Date: _____

_____
_____
_____
_____
_____
_____
_____
_____
_____
_____
_____
_____
_____
_____
_____
_____

I am grateful for _____
_____

Success Journal ©Stacia Pierce

Notes
Date: _____

I am grateful for _____

Success Journal ©Stacia Pierce

Notes

Date: _____

I am grateful for _____

Success Journal ©Stacia Pierce

Notes

Date: _____

I am grateful for _____

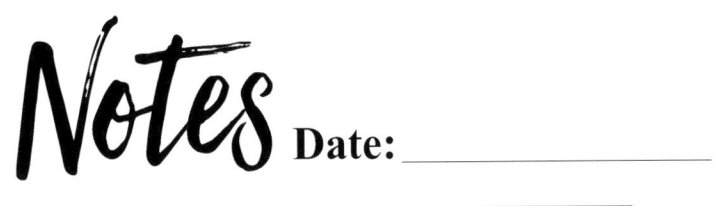

Success Journal ©Stacia Pierce

Notes

Date: _____

I am grateful for _____

When you see it, say it and believe it, you can manifest it.

Let your dreams be bigger than your fears.

Success Journal ©Stacia Pierce

The Big I am

Write a positive affirmation about where you are headed by finishing the statement:

I am...

Meditation Mornings

Week of _____

Take 15 minutes each morning to focus on your day and meditate. Ask God questions regarding your dreams and goals. Afterwards, use the spaces below to write any thoughts and ideas that you hear.

Sunday:

Monday:

Tuesday:

Success Journal ©Stacia Pierce

Wednesday:

Thursday:

Friday:

Saturday:

Success Journal ©Stacia Pierce

Daily Dreams

Week of _____

Take a few minutes each day to focus on your dreams. Ask questions regarding your dreams and goals. Afterwards, use the spaces below to write any dreams that you had the night before.

Sunday:

_____
_____
_____
_____

Monday:

_____
_____
_____
_____

Tuesday:

_____
_____
_____
_____

Success Journal ©Stacia Pierce

Wednesday:

Thursday:

Friday:

Saturday:

Success Journal ©Stacia Pierce

My List

for the week of _____

- [ ] 1.
- [ ] 2.
- [ ] 3.
- [ ] 4.
- [ ] 5.
- [ ] 6.
- [ ] 7.
- [ ] 8.
- [ ] 9.
- [ ] 10.
- [ ] 11.
- [ ] 12.
- [ ] 13.
- [ ] 14.
- [ ] 15.
- [ ] 16.

- [ ] 17.
- [ ] 18.
- [ ] 19.
- [ ] 20.
- [ ] 21.
- [ ] 22.
- [ ] 23.
- [ ] 24.
- [ ] 25.
- [ ] 26.
- [ ] 27.
- [ ] 28.
- [ ] 29.
- [ ] 30.
- [ ] 31.
- [ ] 32.
- [ ] 33.
- [ ] 34.
- [ ] 35.
- [ ] 36.

My Quotes and Affirmations

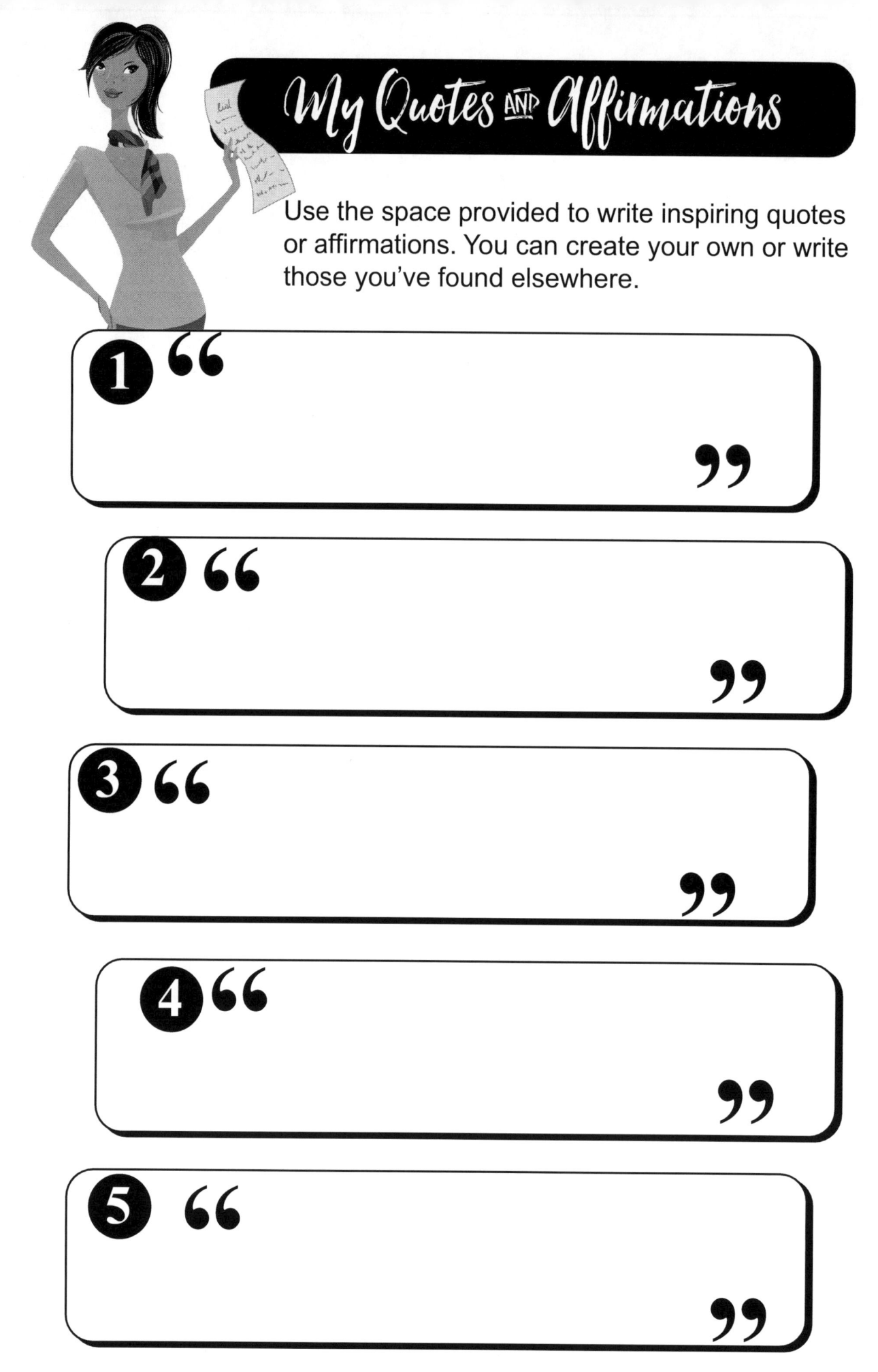

Use the space provided to write inspiring quotes or affirmations. You can create your own or write those you've found elsewhere.

1. " "

2. " "

3. " "

4. " "

5. " "

Success Journal ©Stacia Pierce

6. " "

7. " "

8. " "

9. " "

10. " "

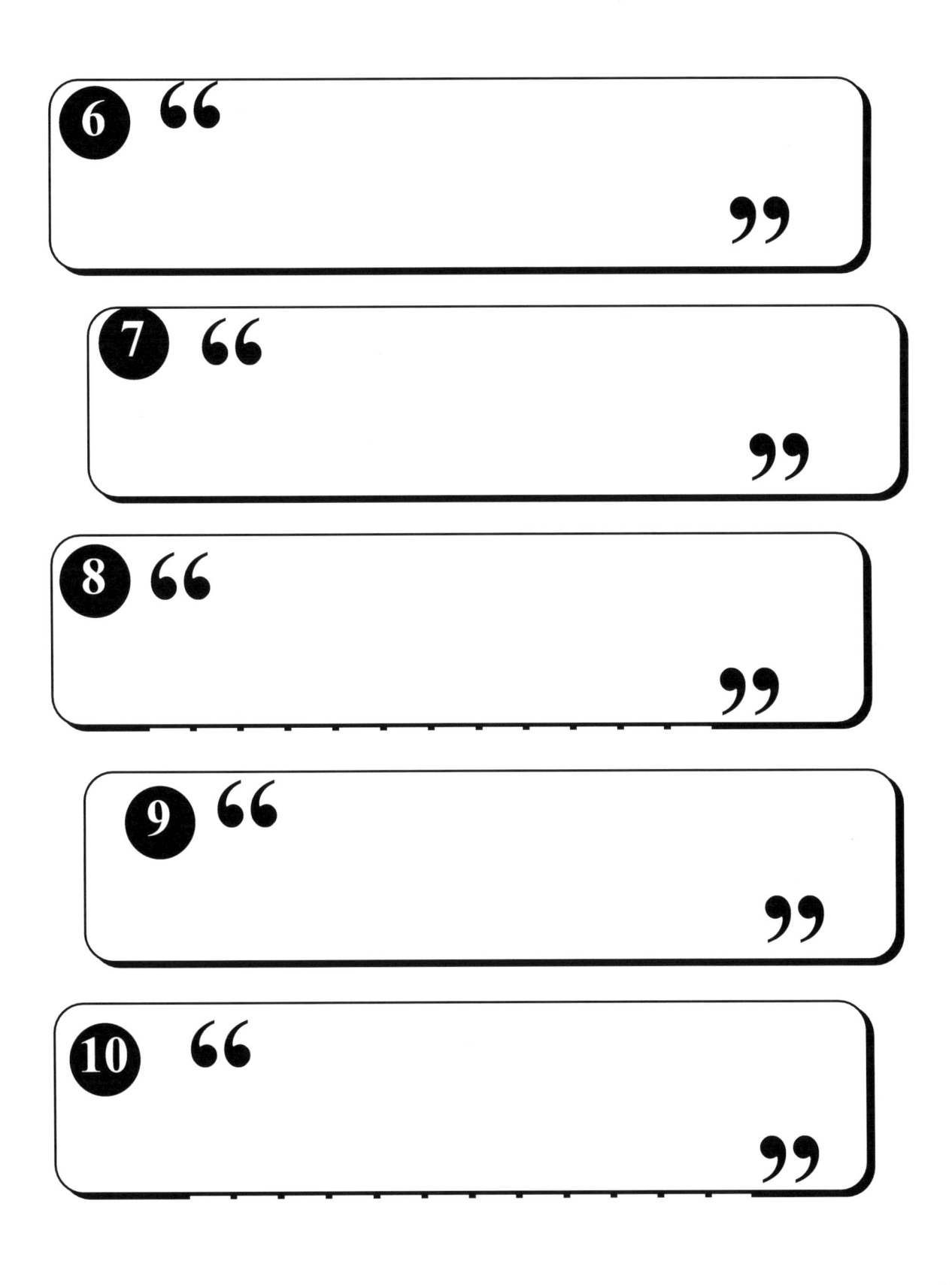

Information changes the seasons of your life.
— **Stacia Pierce**

My Vision Statement
What I see for me.

Write about what's next. What do you see happening this week or in the near future?

Success Journal ©Stacia Pierce

My Vision Board
What I see for me.

Bring your vision statement to life by cutting and pasting pictures and words here.

Manifest Your Money

Write these blank checks to yourself with your current goal income amounts. Keep them here to view during your meditation time or cut them out and post them to view daily.

Unlimited Money Manifestation Bank
777 Believe it & Receive it Avenue
Everywhere, I AM

1111

_____ DATE

$ _____

PAY TO THE ORDER OF _____ DOLLARS

This is a visualization tool from Dr. Stacia and Ariana Pierce

BANK OF WEALTH FOR ME
This is not an instrument subject to Article # of the UCC

FOR _____ Signed: _____

⑆00000 4444⑆ 000000529⑈ 1111   *Imagine, improve, increase.* www.lifecoach2women.com

---

Unlimited Money Manifestation Bank
777 Believe it & Receive it Avenue
Everywhere, I AM

1111

_____ DATE

$ _____

PAY TO THE ORDER OF _____ DOLLARS

This is a visualization tool from Dr. Stacia and Ariana Pierce

BANK OF WEALTH FOR ME
This is not an instrument subject to Article # of the UCC

FOR _____ Signed: _____

⑆00000 4444⑆ 000000529⑈ 1111   *Imagine, improve, increase.* www.lifecoach2women.com

---

Unlimited Money Manifestation Bank
777 Believe it & Receive it Avenue
Everywhere, I AM

1111

_____ DATE

$ _____

PAY TO THE ORDER OF _____ DOLLARS

This is a visualization tool from Dr. Stacia and Ariana Pierce

BANK OF WEALTH FOR ME
This is not an instrument subject to Article # of the UCC

FOR _____ Signed: _____

⑆00000 4444⑆ 000000529⑈ 1111   *Imagine, improve, increase.* www.lifecoach2women.com

Notes
Date:_____

I am grateful for _____

Success Journal ©Stacia Pierce

Notes

Date: _____

_____
_____
_____
_____
_____
_____
_____
_____
_____
_____
_____
_____
_____
_____
_____

I am grateful for _____

_____

Success Journal ©Stacia Pierce

Notes
Date: _____

I am grateful for _____

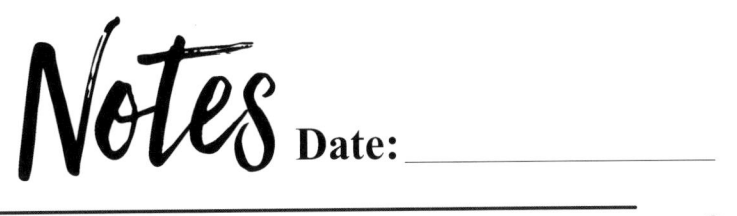

Success Journal ©Stacia Pierce

Notes

Date: _____

I am grateful for _____

Notes
Date: _____

I am grateful for _____

Notes

Date: _____

I am grateful for _____

Success Journal ©Stacia Pierce

Notes
Date: _____

I am grateful for _____

Success Journal ©Stacia Pierce

Notes

Date: _____

I am grateful for _____

Success Journal ©Stacia Pierce

Notes

Date: _____

I am grateful for _____

Notes   Date:

I am grateful for

Success Journal ©Stacia Pierce

Notes

Date: _____

I am grateful for _____

Success Journal ©Stacia Pierce

Notes

Date: _____

I am grateful for _____

Success Journal ©Stacia Pierce

Notes

Date: _____

I am grateful for _____

Success Journal ©Stacia Pierce

Notes

Date: _____

I am grateful for _____

Success Journal ©Stacia Pierce

Notes
Date:_____

I am grateful for _____

Success Journal ©Stacia Pierce

Notes

Date: _____

I am grateful for _____

Success Journal ©Stacia Pierce

Notes

Date: _____

_____
_____
_____
_____
_____
_____
_____
_____
_____
_____
_____
_____
_____
_____

I am grateful for _____
_____

Success Journal ©Stacia Pierce

Notes

Date: _____

I am grateful for _____

Success Journal ©Stacia Pierce

Notes

Date: _____

_____
_____
_____
_____
_____
_____
_____
_____
_____
_____
_____
_____
_____
_____
_____

I am grateful for _____

Success Journal ©Stacia Pierce

Notes

Date: _____

I am grateful for _____

Success Journal ©Stacia Pierce

Notes   Date:_____

_____
_____
_____
_____
_____
_____
_____
_____
_____
_____
_____
_____
_____
_____
_____

I am grateful for _____
_____

Success Journal ©Stacia Pierce

Notes

Date: _____

I am grateful for _____

Success Journal ©Stacia Pierce

Notes
Date: _____

I am grateful for _____

Success Journal ©Stacia Pierce

Notes

Date: _____

I am grateful for _____

Success Journal ©Stacia Pierce

Notes

Date: _____

I am grateful for _____

Success Journal ©Stacia Pierce

Notes

Date: _____

I am grateful for _____

Success Journal ©Stacia Pierce

Notes

Date: _____

I am grateful for _____

Notes

Date: _____

I am grateful for _____

Success Journal ©Stacia Pierce

Notes

Date: _____

I am grateful for _____

Success Journal ©Stacia Pierce

Notes

Date: _____

I am grateful for _____

Notes

Date: _____

I am grateful for _____

Notes

Date: _____

I am grateful for _____

Success Journal ©Stacia Pierce

You will manifest what you meditate on the most!

Success Journal ©Stacia Pierce

What you are seeking, is also seeking you.

Success Journal ©Stacia Pierce

The Big I am

Write a positive affirmation about where you are headed by finishing the statement:

I am...

Meditation Mornings

Week of _____

Take 15 minutes each morning to focus on your day and meditate. Ask God questions regarding your dreams and goals. Afterwards, use the spaces below to write any thoughts and ideas that you hear.

Sunday:

_____
_____
_____
_____

Monday:

_____
_____
_____
_____

Tuesday:

_____
_____
_____
_____

Success Journal ©Stacia Pierce

Wednesday:

Thursday:

Friday:

Saturday:

Success Journal ©Stacia Pierce

Daily Dreams

Week of _____

Take a few minutes each day to focus on your dreams. Ask questions regarding your dreams and goals. Afterwards, use the spaces below to write any dreams that you had the night before.

Sunday:

_____
_____
_____
_____

Monday:

_____
_____
_____
_____

Tuesday:

_____
_____
_____
_____

Success Journal ©Stacia Pierce

Wednesday:

Thursday:

Friday:

Saturday:

Success Journal ©Stacia Pierce

My List

for the week of _____

- [ ] 1.
- [ ] 2.
- [ ] 3.
- [ ] 4.
- [ ] 5.
- [ ] 6.
- [ ] 7.
- [ ] 8.
- [ ] 9.
- [ ] 10.
- [ ] 11.
- [ ] 12.
- [ ] 13.
- [ ] 14.
- [ ] 15.
- [ ] 16.

- [ ] **17.**
- [ ] **18.**
- [ ] **19.**
- [ ] **20.**
- [ ] **21.**
- [ ] **22.**
- [ ] **23.**
- [ ] **24.**
- [ ] **25.**
- [ ] **26.**
- [ ] **27.**
- [ ] **28.**
- [ ] **29.**
- [ ] **30.**
- [ ] **31.**
- [ ] **32.**
- [ ] **33.**
- [ ] **34.**
- [ ] **35.**
- [ ] **36.**

My Quotes and Affirmations

Use the space provided to write inspiring quotes or affirmations. You can create your own or write those you've found elsewhere.

1. " "

2. " "

3. " "

4. " "

5. " "

Success Journal ©Stacia Pierce

6 " "

7 " "

8 " "

9 " "

10 " "

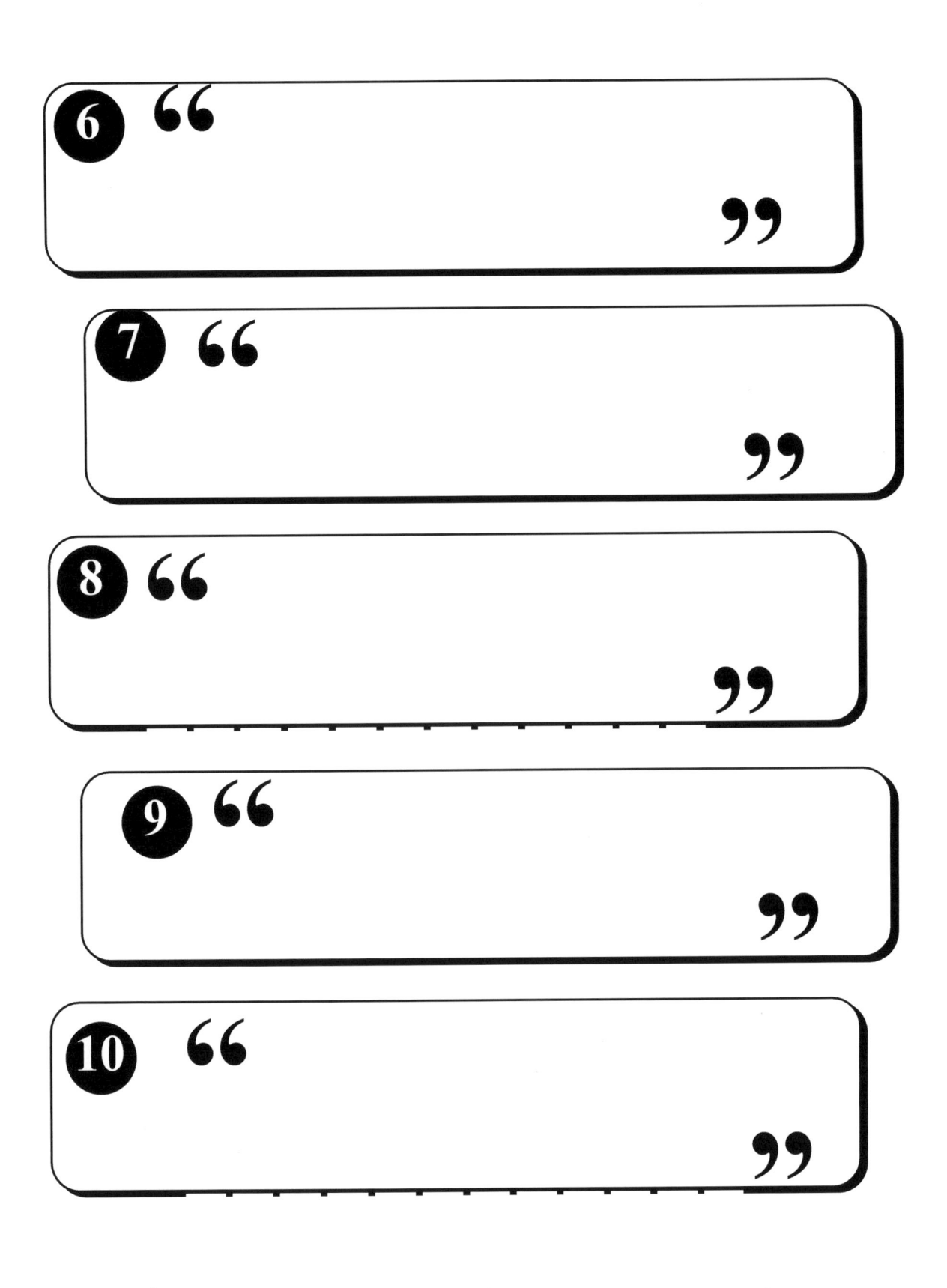

Information changes the seasons of your life.
— **Stacia Pierce**

Success Journal ©Stacia Pierce

My Vision Statement
What I see for me.

Write about what's next. What do you see happening this week or in the near future?

Success Journal ©Stacia Pierce

My Vision Board
What I see for me.

Bring your vision statement to life by cutting and pasting pictures and words here.

Success Journal ©Stacia Pierce

Manifest Your Money

Write these blank checks to yourself with your current goal income amounts. Keep them here to view during your meditation time or cut them out and post them to view daily.

Unlimited Money Manifestation Bank
777 Believe it & Receive it Avenue
Everywhere, I AM

1111

DATE _____

$ _____

PAY TO THE ORDER OF _____ DOLLARS

This is a visualization tool from Dr. Stacia and Ariana Pierce

BANK OF WEALTH FOR ME
This is not an instrument subject to Article # of the UCC

FOR _____ Signed: _____

⑆000004444⑆ 000000529⑈ 1111   *imagine. improve. increase.*   www.lifecoach2women.com

---

Unlimited Money Manifestation Bank
777 Believe it & Receive it Avenue
Everywhere, I AM

1111

DATE _____

$ _____

PAY TO THE ORDER OF _____ DOLLARS

This is a visualization tool from Dr. Stacia and Ariana Pierce

BANK OF WEALTH FOR ME
This is not an instrument subject to Article # of the UCC

FOR _____ Signed: _____

⑆000004444⑆ 000000529⑈ 1111   *imagine. improve. increase.*   www.lifecoach2women.com

---

Unlimited Money Manifestation Bank
777 Believe it & Receive it Avenue
Everywhere, I AM

1111

DATE _____

$ _____

PAY TO THE ORDER OF _____ DOLLARS

This is a visualization tool from Dr. Stacia and Ariana Pierce

BANK OF WEALTH FOR ME
This is not an instrument subject to Article # of the UCC

FOR _____ Signed: _____

⑆000004444⑆ 000000529⑈ 1111   *imagine. improve. increase.*   www.lifecoach2women.com

Notes
Date:_____

I am grateful for _____

Success Journal ©Stacia Pierce

Notes Date: _____

_____
_____
_____
_____
_____
_____
_____
_____
_____
_____
_____
_____
_____
_____

I am grateful for _____
_____

Success Journal ©Stacia Pierce

Notes Date:_____

I am grateful for _____

Success Journal ©Stacia Pierce

Notes

Date: _____

I am grateful for _____

Success Journal ©Stacia Pierce

Notes Date:

I am grateful for

Notes

Date: _____

I am grateful for _____

Success Journal ©Stacia Pierce

Notes
Date: _____

I am grateful for _____

Notes

Date: _____

I am grateful for _____

Success Journal ©Stacia Pierce

Notes
Date:_____

I am grateful for _____

Notes

Date: _____

I am grateful for _____

Notes
Date:_____

I am grateful for _____

Notes

Date: _____

_____
_____
_____
_____
_____
_____
_____
_____
_____
_____
_____
_____
_____
_____
_____
_____
_____
_____

I am grateful for _____
_____

Notes

Date: _____

I am grateful for _____

Notes

Date: _____

I am grateful for _____

Success Journal ©Stacia Pierce

Notes

Date: _____

I am grateful for _____

Success Journal ©Stacia Pierce

Notes

Date: _____

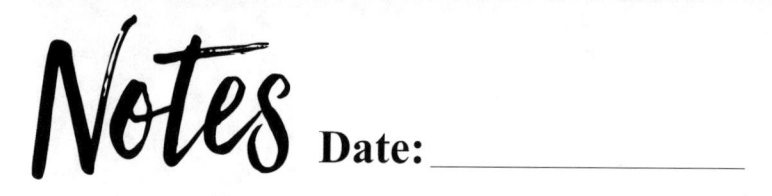

I am grateful for _____

Success Journal ©Stacia Pierce

Notes

Date: _____

I am grateful for _____

Success Journal ©Stacia Pierce

Notes

Date: _____

I am grateful for _____

Success Journal ©Stacia Pierce

Notes
Date:_____

I am grateful for _____

Success Journal ©Stacia Pierce

Notes

Date: _____

I am grateful for _____

Success Journal ©Stacia Pierce

Notes

Date: _____

I am grateful for _____

Success Journal ©Stacia Pierce

Notes

Date: _____

I am grateful for _____

Notes Date: _____

I am grateful for _____

Success Journal ©Stacia Pierce

Notes

Date: _____

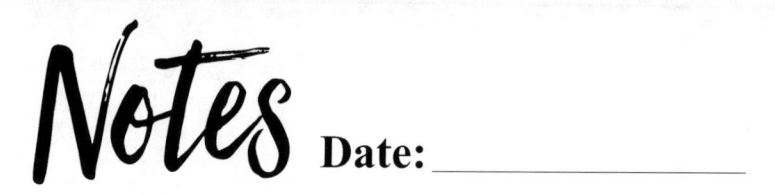

I am grateful for _____

Success Journal ©Stacia Pierce

Notes

Date: _____

I am grateful for _____
_____

Notes

Date: _____

I am grateful for _____

Success Journal ©Stacia Pierce

Notes
Date: _____

I am grateful for _____

Success Journal ©Stacia Pierce

Notes

Date: _____

I am grateful for _____

Success Journal ©Stacia Pierce

Notes
Date:_____

I am grateful for _____

Success Journal ©Stacia Pierce

Notes

Date: _____

I am grateful for _____

Success Journal ©Stacia Pierce

Notes Date:_____

I am grateful for _____

Notes Date: _____

_____
_____
_____
_____
_____
_____
_____
_____
_____
_____
_____
_____
_____
_____
_____
_____

I am grateful for _____
_____

Success Journal ©Stacia Pierce

The power of imagination makes us limitless.

Always expect that something wonderful will happen.

Success Journal ©Stacia Pierce

The Big I am

Write a positive affirmation about where you are headed by finishing the statement:

I am...

Meditation Mornings

Week of _____

Take 15 minutes each morning to focus on your day and meditate. Ask God questions regarding your dreams and goals. Afterwards, use the spaces below to write any thoughts and ideas that you hear.

Sunday:
_____
_____
_____
_____

Monday:
_____
_____
_____
_____

Tuesday:
_____
_____
_____
_____

Success Journal ©Stacia Pierce

Wednesday:

Thursday:

Friday:

Saturday:

Success Journal ©Stacia Pierce

Daily Dreams

Week of _____

Take a few minutes each day to focus on your dreams. Ask questions regarding your dreams and goals. Afterwards, use the spaces below to write any dreams that you had the night before.

Sunday:
_____
_____
_____
_____

Monday:
_____
_____
_____
_____

Tuesday:
_____
_____
_____
_____

Success Journal ©Stacia Pierce

Wednesday:

Thursday:

Friday:

Saturday:

Success Journal ©Stacia Pierce

My List

for the week of _____

☐ 1.

☐ 2.

☐ 3.

☐ 4.

☐ 5.

☐ 6.

☐ 7.

☐ 8.

☐ 9.

☐ 10.

☐ 11.

☐ 12.

☐ 13.

☐ 14.

☐ 15.

☐ 16.

☐ 17.

☐ 18.

☐ 19.

☐ 20.

☐ 21.

☐ 22.

☐ 23.

☐ 24.

☐ 25.

☐ 26.

☐ 27.

☐ 28.

☐ 29.

☐ 30.

☐ 31.

☐ 32.

☐ 33.

☐ 34.

☐ 35.

☐ 36.

My Quotes and Affirmations

Use the space provided to write inspiring quotes or affirmations. You can create your own or write those you've found elsewhere.

1. " "

2. " "

3. " "

4. " "

5. " "

Success Journal ©Stacia Pierce

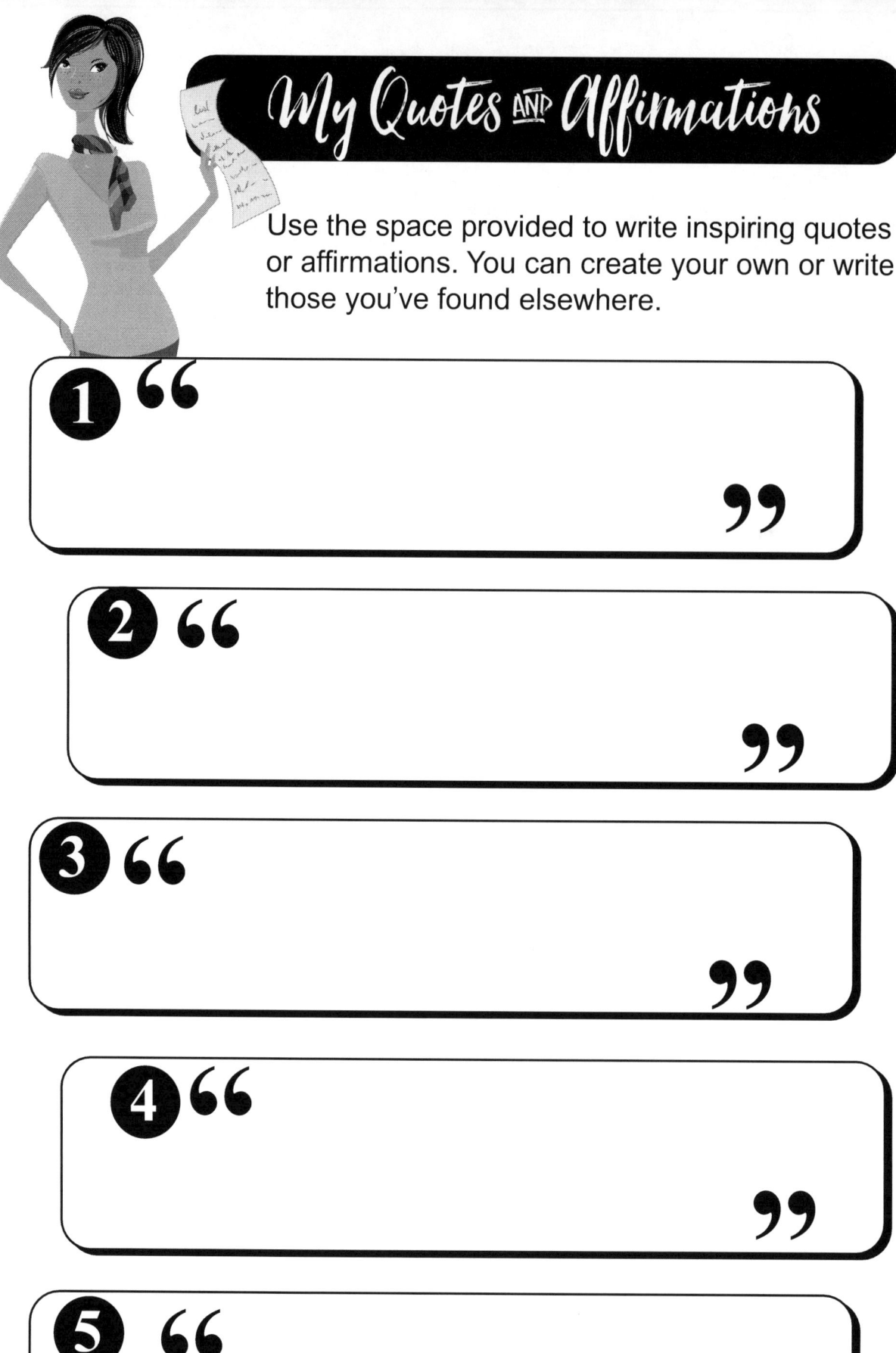

6 " "

7 " "

8 " "

9 " "

10 " "

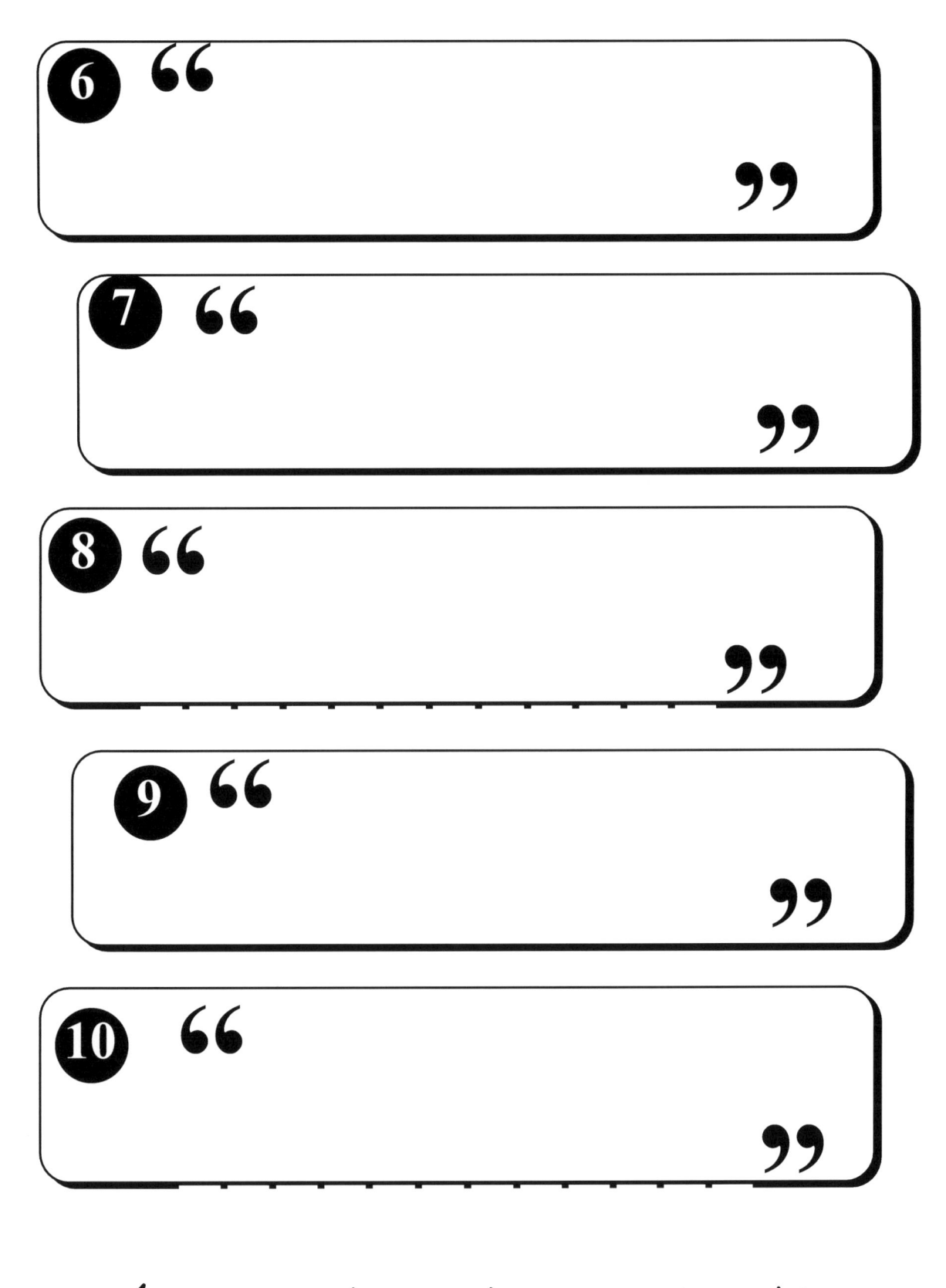

Information changes the seasons of your life.
- Stacia Pierce

My Vision Statement
What I see for me.

Write about what's next. What do you see happening this week or in the near future?

Success Journal ©Stacia Pierce

My Vision Board
What I see for me.

Bring your vision statement to life by cutting and pasting pictures and words here.

Success Journal ©Stacia Pierce

Manifest Your Money

Write these blank checks to yourself with your current goal income amounts. Keep them here to view during your meditation time or cut them out and post them to view daily.

Unlimited Money Manifestation Bank
777 Believe it & Receive it Avenue
Everywhere, I AM

1111

DATE _____

$ _____

PAY TO THE ORDER OF _____ DOLLARS

This is a visualization tool from Dr. Stacia and Ariana Pierce

BANK OF WEALTH FOR ME
This is not an instrument subject to Article # of the UCC

FOR _____ Signed: _____

⑆00000 4444⑆ 000000 529⑈ 1111   *imagine. improve. increase.* www.lifecoach2women.com

---

Unlimited Money Manifestation Bank
777 Believe it & Receive it Avenue
Everywhere, I AM

1111

DATE _____

$ _____

PAY TO THE ORDER OF _____ DOLLARS

This is a visualization tool from Dr. Stacia and Ariana Pierce

BANK OF WEALTH FOR ME
This is not an instrument subject to Article # of the UCC

FOR _____ Signed: _____

⑆00000 4444⑆ 000000 529⑈ 1111   *imagine. improve. increase.* www.lifecoach2women.com

---

Unlimited Money Manifestation Bank
777 Believe it & Receive it Avenue
Everywhere, I AM

1111

DATE _____

$ _____

PAY TO THE ORDER OF _____ DOLLARS

This is a visualization tool from Dr. Stacia and Ariana Pierce

BANK OF WEALTH FOR ME
This is not an instrument subject to Article # of the UCC

FOR _____ Signed: _____

⑆00000 4444⑆ 000000 529⑈ 1111   *imagine. improve. increase.* www.lifecoach2women.com

Notes

Date: _____

I am grateful for _____

Notes

Date: _____

I am grateful for _____

Success Journal ©Stacia Pierce

Notes   Date: _____

_____
_____
_____
_____
_____
_____
_____
_____
_____
_____
_____
_____
_____
_____
_____

I am grateful for _____
_____

Success Journal ©Stacia Pierce

Notes

Date: _____

I am grateful for _____

Success Journal ©Stacia Pierce

Notes
Date: _____

I am grateful for _____

Success Journal ©Stacia Pierce

Notes

Date: _____

I am grateful for _____

Success Journal ©Stacia Pierce

Notes

Date: _____

_____
_____
_____
_____
_____
_____
_____
_____
_____
_____
_____
_____
_____
_____

I am grateful for _____
_____

Notes

Date: _____

I am grateful for _____

Success Journal ©Stacia Pierce

Notes Date:_____

I am grateful for _____

Success Journal ©Stacia Pierce

Notes

Date: _____

I am grateful for _____

Success Journal ©Stacia Pierce

Notes
Date: _____

I am grateful for _____

Success Journal ©Stacia Pierce

Notes

Date: _____

I am grateful for _____

Success Journal ©Stacia Pierce

Notes Date:_____

I am grateful for _____

Notes

Date: _____

I am grateful for _____

Notes Date: _____

I am grateful for _____

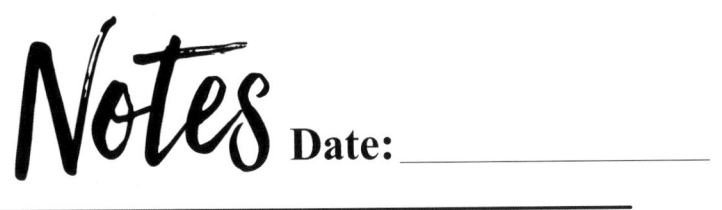

Success Journal ©Stacia Pierce

Notes

Date: _____

I am grateful for _____

Success Journal ©Stacia Pierce

Notes Date:

I am grateful for

Success Journal ©Stacia Pierce

Notes

Date: _____

I am grateful for _____

Success Journal ©Stacia Pierce

Notes   Date:_____

_____
_____
_____
_____
_____
_____
_____
_____
_____
_____
_____
_____
_____
_____
_____
_____

I am grateful for _____
_____

Success Journal ©Stacia Pierce

Notes

Date: _____

I am grateful for _____

Notes
Date: _____

I am grateful for _____

Success Journal ©Stacia Pierce

Notes

Date: _____

I am grateful for _____

Success Journal ©Stacia Pierce

Notes

Date: _____

I am grateful for _____

Success Journal ©Stacia Pierce

Notes

Date: _____

I am grateful for _____

Success Journal ©Stacia Pierce

Notes

Date: _____

I am grateful for _____

Success Journal ©Stacia Pierce

Notes

Date: _____

I am grateful for _____

Success Journal ©Stacia Pierce

Notes
Date: _____

I am grateful for _____

Success Journal ©Stacia Pierce

Notes

Date: _____

I am grateful for _____

Success Journal ©Stacia Pierce

Notes
Date: _____

I am grateful for _____

Success Journal ©Stacia Pierce

Notes

Date: _____

I am grateful for _____

Success Journal ©Stacia Pierce

Notes

Date: _____

I am grateful for _____

Notes

Date: _____

I am grateful for _____

Success Journal ©Stacia Pierce

Notes
Date:_____

I am grateful for _____

Notes Date: _____

_____
_____
_____
_____
_____
_____
_____
_____
_____
_____
_____
_____
_____
_____
_____
_____
_____
_____

I am grateful for _____
_____

The POWER of JOURNALING

The million-dollar manifestation prompts, props, notes and guided steps to manifest a millionaire lifestyle.

Success Journal ©Stacia Pierce

…

7 Tips for POWERFUL Intentional Journaling

Over the years I have been very intentional about keeping a journal and writing lists. My writing practices have literally caused me to be able to change my life, business and manifest dreams I once had only inside. I got a hold of the secret of writing your way to success long ago and created this success journal as a tool to help others do the same.

The following pages share my guided notes, prompts worksheets and props to help you rev up your manifestation process. My Success Journal Workshop or Manifest 10 Fold Master Class will give you much more detail, but here are a few of my favorite tips and practices for daily journaling.

1. Date your entries in your journal
It makes it easier to reference your notes when you are capturing ideas and thoughts in motion each day.

2. Keep a dream log
Record your night dreams first thing in the morning. God is not required to repeat Himself!

3. Ask God questions in your journal
If you ask, you'll get an answer. Write out what solutions came to you. Often, answers can come throughout the day or will come from somebody around you.

4. Keep a daily IDEA list in your journal
SYSTEMATICALLY DOCUMENT all of your ideas for the NEXT 30 DAYS. Carry around your journal and write down every little idea that comes to you. Choose which ones to take action on and go! Take action towards your dream daily.

5. Be sure to write your 101 goals in your journal
I believe in truly DREAMING BIG, DREAMS AND GOING BIG. The more goals you have the more goals you'll end up achieving.

6. Record your systems, processes and procedures
Note the systems, processes and procedures that you are currently performing. Also make record of what you perfect. In the early years, as I was rapidly growing my company, I started recording any simple step by step process that I used to get things done. Those notes turned into coaching women, creating workshops, tele-seminars and podcasts. Writing blog posts, new books, operating manuals and company manuals. Every thing I've created started in my journals-- and they've all turned into big increase and profits!

7. List your life in your Success Journal
I truly live by lists. My productivity routine is list writing. Make a list of achievable items you want to get done for the week and month. WHEN I'M LOOKING FOR ANSWERS to something I don't know, I WRITE OUT A LIST of things I want to find answers to. And guess what? The answers always show up!

This is just the tip of the iceberg, however I have practiced each and every one of these journaling techniques in my life and they have caused me major manifestations.

Success Journal ©Stacia Pierce

My Manifestation LIST

What you want wants you too. It's just a matter of you shifting your mindset and perception of what's possible so you can receive it. Hide away for a few moments, sit quietly, get clear and use this page to list what you want to manifest in your business and life right now.

Right now I desire to manifest...

1. _____
2. _____
3. _____
4. _____
5. _____
6. _____
7. _____
8. _____
9. _____
10. _____

Notes:

_____
_____
_____
_____
_____

Success Journal ©Stacia Pierce

My Luxurious Life List

What does living your luxurious life require? What elements/routines/activities do you need to add to your life, to enjoy life and feel amazing while doing so?

Do you need fresh flowers in your home weekly, perfume on your bathroom counter? Maybe you love your car impeccably cleaned with a delightful scent?

Do you desire to have your hair, nails and pedicures done weekly? A wardrobe of designer purses? Whatever your lux life requires, list it below.

Place Your Photo Here

My Luxurious Life

1. _____
2. _____
3. _____
4. _____
5. _____
6. _____
7. _____
8. _____
9. _____
10. _____
11. _____
12. _____
13. _____
14. _____
15. _____

Success Journal ©Stacia Pierce

How to Write
My Best Life Script

WHAT IS A BEST LIFE SCRIPT?

Scripting your life for success is real. Journaling and scripting what you desire attracts what you want to you. Your journal can be your prosperity plan. Your journal is where you document your sparks of ideas or your outcome as if it happened. Journaling your best life script is a little different than your regular daily journal entry. It's taking a bit of time to stop and really think about the kind of life you want to live, who you want to become, the relationships you want to have, the income you want to create, the impact you want to make, and the legacy you'd like to leave behind. As you ponder those things and get clarity on the life that you want to create, then you create a script to reflect the life you desire. I've broken the process down into four simple steps:

1. Think it all through. When you journalize your best life script, consider what you really want your ideal outcome to be for your life and business before you start writing in your journal. Get quiet and listen to your heart. What are your true desires? Ask yourself: "What do I really want?" Then sit in silence and listen within for the answers to some of the following questions:

How do I want to live?
How much money do I want to make?
What legacy do I want to leave for my family?
What do I want my relationships to be like?
How do I want my business to grow?
What kind of cars do I want to drive?
Jot down a few notes here:
What do I want my health to be like?

_____
_____
_____
_____
_____
_____
_____
_____
_____
_____
_____
_____
_____
_____
_____
_____
_____
_____
_____
_____

Success Journal ©Stacia Pierce

Write a few notes here:

_____

_____

Simply imagine your best life as a whole; then begin to journalize. Write out your life exactly how you want to live it. Don't hold back just pour your heart onto the pages of your Success Journal.

2. Journalize your best life script as if you are already living the life that you want to live.
Instead of writing things like: "One day I will have…" or "I will be…" Write in present tense with statements that sound more like… "I'm so grateful and thankful for my beautiful home that…"
Write your life script as if…
You're already enjoying the new home that you want to live in.
- *You're enjoying your new relationship.*
- *You've already received a Grammy for your music.*
- *Your book has just hit the best sellers list.*
- *You are already driving the car that you want.*
- *You already have the top clientele that you wanted*
- *You're already bringing in the monthly income you desired*

3. Journalize your best life script using vibrant, positive words.
For example, in lieu of writing, *"I'm so tired of my situation right now, I'm totally getting out of debt this year!"*
Write with happy words that make you feel great.

When you use words like tired, debt, etc. it's still bringing negativity into your manifestation space. You don't want debt or exhaustion so don't give any attention to them. What you focus on you will manifest, good or bad.

Make no mention of what you don't want ONLY state what you want. So you could write instead… "I am overjoyed that I live in a constant state of abundance. I'm so excited about my outstanding clients they adore my products and services and are raving fans." Same concept, sans the negativity.

4. Connect yourself emotionally to your life script. Write from your heart not just your head.
Think about what's most important to you so that you can truly connect to the emotion of living this life you've seen in your minds eye. The best way to connect to the emotion of your best life script is to really think about how you'll feel when the goal is manifested and incorporate those emotions into your writing.

A normal entry might say *"I'm thankful for my new, luxury car."*
A more emotionally connected entry would be, " I adore my new car. I'm proud of the work I've done and feel so very blessed that I'm driving my _____. I love my plush seats and that it's my favorite color. I smile every time I drive it—I feel so rewarded for the work I put in to get it."

The more you're able to feel the emotion of manifesting your desired outcome, the more effective you'll be at attracting it. Though journaling your best life script is truly a powerful practice, it doesn't have to take a long time to execute. **Set aside twenty to thirty minutes in the next 24 hours to write your first draft in your journal.**

Success Journal ©Stacia Pierce

Writing Your Best Life Script

Life Script Starter Phrases

Now that you have the steps to write your script take a moment to sit and think. What is your big dream right now? Think about the one big goal that you want to manifest.

What do you want to have?
What do you want to do?
What do you want to become?
Where do you want to go?

Use the next page to write out your best life script. Here are a few starter phrases to get you started:

■ I am abundantly wealthy. I am so grateful and thankful that I have $_____ yearly income and my net-worth is $_____

■ I am so grateful and thankful that I am in great health and live in a very happy, long life.

■ I am so happy and grateful that I have a loving spouse and we are completely in love with one another and together we enjoy a wealthy, happy, healthy, long life.

■ I am living in my brand new (built from the ground up or move-in ready) home. I love every square foot of my beautiful, luxurious, well equipped, custom living space.

■ I love my life work/business. I am so excited and grateful to be in the BIG MONEY FLOW. I get money ideas for increase in my sleep, in my meditation time, in my journaling time, in my brainstorming time, in my coaching time, in my mastermind time.

■ I am so delighted about my new vehicle it's a _____

Success Journal ©Stacia Pierce

My Best Life Script

The Power of Wealth Journaling

Wealth journaling is my go-to method when in the process of solving money challenges or…if I'm simply in the mood to take my finances to the next level. Your best life script is for your life overall, wealth journaling is focusing specifically on financial increase. Every time I'm ready to manifest increase in my personal life or through my business, wealth journaling has saved the day. *I'm going to show you how you can use this for a specific financial need or for your manifestation of wealth overall. Here are my six steps to manifest through wealth journaling.*

1. Write out your specific request/desired outcome.
Whenever I'm in wealth journaling mode, I write a freestyle morning script of the specific financial outcome I want to manifest in my life. I always write in present or past tense. This is a technique to train your brain to do what you want. If you're writing in the future, then you'll stay in a state of wanting something to happen vs. writing in the present where it's currently happening or in the past where it has already happened for you. When wealth journaling the more specific the better while you are scripting your desired outcome.

For example, if you are expanding your business and need to hire an assistant but don't quite have the extra funds. You may start by writing something like… "I'm so grateful and thankful that I found the perfect assistant! Her skills and personality are a wonderful fit for this company and me. I'm able to pay her well with ease and her efforts here immediately bring increase to my bottom line…"

What is your specific wealth request? What do you want to manifest?
_____
_____
_____

Success Journal ©Stacia Pierce

What is your daily sales goal?
_____

What is your monthly income goal?
_____

2. Create an affirmation in line with your desired outcome.
* Take 20-30 minutes journaling about what you want to happen in your life and in your business/finances this year.

* Now that you have an idea of what you want and have noted the keywords and phrases that stand out to you, it's time to write your mantra. Tips for writing your mantra:
* Remember to keep it short and to the point.
* Keep all aspects of your mantra positive. For example, instead of saying, "I will stop being lazy and unproductive so I can make more money." INSTEAD Say, "I am diligent, productive and my income continually increases as a result."

* Keep it in present tense as if good things are happening right now, not in the future.

* Write your mantra below. For example, here is one of my Money Mantras: *"I accept and allow all abundance, fulfillment and happiness to continue to flow in my life right now. Everything and everyone prospers me now. Every day in every way!"*

_____
_____
_____
_____
_____

• Be sure to repeat this mantra at least 3 times daily or whenever it comes to you as you are thinking about your finances.
• This mantra doesn't have to be kept for the whole year. Keep it as long as it resonates with you and update it as needed.
• When repeating your mantra, say it with passion and feeling. See yourself living out the words that you are speaking.

3. Remember to practice gratitude daily.
Wealthy, happy people have mastered the art of being grateful for what they have while they are on their way to where they want to be. **Keep track of all increase.** If you're given anything, keep note of the monetary amount you saved by receiving the gift. This will cause you to be intentionally grateful. At the conclusion of each of your wealth journaling sessions list what financial blessings you are grateful for right now.

Success Journal ©Stacia Pierce

MY MONEY
Tracker

A key to generating more income is to acknowledge, track and be grateful for all of the increase that has already come your way. This sheet will help you recognize and track all of the various ways you received income this week.

Today's Date: _____

BUSINESS/WORK INCREASE $ AMOUNT

1. _____   _____
2. _____   _____
3. _____   _____
4. _____   _____
5. _____   _____
6. _____   _____
7. _____   _____
8. _____   _____
9. _____   _____
10. _____   _____

ADDITIONAL PAYMENTS, GIFTS, FAVOR

Did someone buy you a coffee, pay for lunch, take care of your traveling expenses? Was a debt canceled or credit extended to you? That all counts as increase. List them below.

1. _____   _____
2. _____   _____
3. _____   _____
4. _____   _____
5. _____   _____
6. _____   _____
7. _____   _____
8. _____   _____
9. _____   _____
10. _____   _____

TOTAL INCREASE FOR THIS WEEK $ _____

Say this Today:
People love to give me money!

Manifestation Affirmation

Your words create your world. Use this two part affirmation to help you manifest great increase in your life. These are the affirmations I used to manifest $100,000. However, feel free to fill in any amount that you desire to manifest. Remember, you can manifest a $100,000 day, $100,000 month or $100,000 year.

It's also very important to meditate on your desired outcome every day. To help you get a detailed vision and keep it at the forefront of your mind here are a few suggestions. Get some play money and post right next to your affirmations or on your goal card. I keep my affirmations embellished with play money on my bathroom mirror, on my night stand and in the flap of my Success Journal.

Money Manifestation Affirmation

Say this 3x daily

- I am manifesting $100K in my life right now.
- Everyday in every way, everything prospers me now.
- I have $100,000 months, weeks and days.
- I have witty inventions and creative ideas that produce massive amounts of wealth for me.
- My products and services are solving problems of people who are willing to pay!
- My ideal clients call me daily, email me often, visit my website and make purchases all the time.
- I have $100,000 in my bank account, just sitting there waiting for me to decide what I want to do with it.
- More and more increase is coming my way, every day in every way.
- I prosper everything and everyone now.
- Everything and everyone prospers me now!
- Thank you God for this or something better already manifested in my life!

Say this once each day

- I am rich with creative ideas.
- I have great ideas that make me lots of money.
- I will share my skills, abilities and talents with others for a price so that I can manifest more abundance.
- I provide massive value to a massive amount of people who pay me massively.
- God provides me with lots of opportunities to do what I love and get paid for it.
- My business attracts lots and lots of people.
- I have an over flow of people lining up to get my products and services.
- I always know what to sell, when to sell it and how to promote it for profits.
- Money comes into my life at a high rapid speed.
- I attract people into my life that pay easily and effortlessly.
- Successful people surround me.
- Good news is coming. A breakthrough is coming in the next 24 hours, something good manifests for me.
- I make enough money to explore life, to travel good, eat good and enjoy life.
- I release all fear of spending money and investing in myself.
- Blessings are flowing now. Great things are flooding in.
- Money flows in large quantities right into my bank account and into my hands.
- Money is always coming.
- Money comes to me from all over the place everyday.
- The money flow never stops, the money just keeps coming and coming.
- Money cometh to me now.
- I check my balances and they keep increasing every time.
- I am so excited and grateful to be in the BIG MONEY FLOW.
- I get money ideas for increase in my sleep, in my meditation time, in my journaling time, in my brain-storming time, in my coaching time, in my mastermind time.
- I keep finding money all over the place. I keep finding ways to increase my money and save more money!

© • Stacia Pierce • Ultimate Lifestyle Enterprises, LLC
4630 S. Kirkman Rd. #343 Orlando, FL 32811 United States (888) 484-7543

Fast Action for Manifestation

Once your life scripts and lists are written it's time to get into manifestation mode. As you review your script and meditate on it. "To-do's" will come to you. Be diligent and take fast action on moving your dream forward. What actions can you take to accelerate the manifestation process? Write them below.

Action Step

Action Step

Action Step

Success Journal ©Stacia Pierce

Manifestation
Worksheets and Props
for
SUCCESSFUL JOURNALING

Success Journal ©Stacia Pierce

My MANIFESTATION Worksheet

I AM so grateful and thankful that I manifested my **IDEAL MATE!**

PLACE YOUR PHOTO HERE

Manifesting My New Spouse

* Remember to state everything in a positive and present tense
Stop for 5-10 minutes and visualize what it would feel like to spend time with your mate. Allow yourself to feel all of the emotions. Now write below what your ideal day is like with your mate:

___

Attracting the love of someone else starts with loving yourself. How will you consistently practice self-care and love as you embark on this manifestation journey?

___

To manifest our deepest desires we must be clear on what we want. Write a list of what you desire in an your ideal mate. This is not a list of strict rules, but rather an honest description of what you want. End your description with the phrase " I'm so grateful for this or something better."

1. _____
2. _____
3. _____
4. _____
5. _____
6. _____
7. _____
8. _____
9. _____
10. _____
11. _____
12. _____
13. _____
14. _____
15. _____
16. _____
17. _____
18. _____
19. _____
20. _____
21. _____
22. _____
23. _____
24. _____
25. _____

My MANIFESTATION Worksheet

I AM so grateful and thankful that I manifested **My NEW HOUSE!**

PLACE YOUR PHOTO HERE

Manifesting My New House

* Remember to state everything in a positive and present tense

Where my new house is located?
_____

What city would I love to live in? _____
What neighborhood? _____
What style of home is it Ranch, Craftsman, Tudor, Colonial or Cape Cod etc.
_____

How many bedrooms? _____
How many bathrooms? _____

Describe the landscaping:
_____
_____
_____
_____

Describe the decor:
_____
_____
_____

More about the decor

_____
_____
_____
_____
_____

What do you want the feel of your home to be?

_____
_____
_____
_____
_____

How do you feel every time you walk in the door?

_____
_____
_____
_____
_____

How do you and your family enjoy your home?

_____
_____
_____
_____
_____

Place more photos of your new home here

My MANIFESTATION Worksheet

I AM so grateful and thankful that I manifested **better HEALTH & WEIGHT LOSS!**

PLACE YOUR PHOTO HERE

Manifesting better Health & Weight Loss
* Remember to state everything in a positive and present tense
Describe the new healthier you. How will you improve your mindset for this journey? What new healthy habits will you add?

_____
_____
_____
_____

What is your ideal weight?_____ By what date do you want to reach this weight?_____
What's your "WHY" for losing weight/Improving your health?

_____
_____
_____

Are you prepared with a weight loss plan/program? If so explain it.

_____
_____

Here are some great things to say daily: *I lose weight naturally. I am losing weight every day. I enjoy eating healthy foods. I love being active to get my body moving every day. I enjoy taking care of my body. I find it easy to maintain my ideal weight. I choose healthy snacks over junk food. I love eating fruits and veggies. I enjoy drinking the proper amount of water for me daily. I deserve to be healthy and in good shape.*

My MANIFESTATION Worksheet

I AM so grateful and thankful that I manifested a **NEW CAR!**

[PLACE YOUR PHOTO HERE]

Manifesting My New Car

* Remember to state everything in a positive and present tense
What's your ideal day like in your new car? _____
_____
_____
_____
_____

What is the color? _____
What is the make and model? _____

Describe how much fun it was to purchase your car:
_____
_____
_____

How do you feel when you're driving your new car?
_____
_____
_____

What kind of road trips do you take in your new car?
_____
_____

My MANIFESTATION Worksheet

I AM so grateful and thankful that I manifested my **FINANCIALLY FREE LIFESTYLE!**

PLACE YOUR PHOTO HERE

Manifesting My Financial Freedom

* Remember to state everything in a positive and present tense

What amount of money/income do I need to manifest monthly to be financially free? _____

Describe your ideal day in your financially free life. What would you do if you had no restraints due to finances, traditional work hours or any lack of resources:

_____
_____
_____
_____
_____
_____
_____
_____
_____
_____
_____
_____
_____
_____
_____
_____
_____
_____

Visualize Your Success with Manifestation Props

When using any of the props and tools provided here within your Success Journal, powering up your **visualization** process is essential. Mental money blocks or varied circumstances can sometimes fog your ability to imagine a detailed picture of you receiving what you've asked for.

However, the thing is that actually SEEING yourself having what you desire is one of the most important steps to manifestation. That's why using tools like the visualization page in your Success Journal, blank checks, or deposit slips (just to name a few) are vital. To manifest big YOU MUST be able to wrap your mind around the fact that you can actually receive what you've asked for. You have to SEE yourself depositing that money. You must SEE yourself living out the life that your bank deposits create. The following pages will provide you with a few props to help you clearly visualize the dreams your are trying to manifest. Pull out and post up your props where you will see them often; or keep them all in your journal in one place. Whatever works best for you but be sure to look at them daily.

2 VIP tickets

You now have 2 VIP tickets to: _____

Now describe below how and why you've received these very special tickets

_____
_____
_____
_____
_____
_____
_____
_____

ADMIT ONE — VIP ENTRANCE
№ 56482314
EVENT: _____
DATE: _____ LOCATION: _____
*NON-TRANSFERRABLE *VALID FOR UNLIMITED RENTRY

ADMIT ONE — VIP ENTRANCE
№ 87351297
EVENT: _____
DATE: _____ LOCATION: _____
*NON-TRANSFERRABLE *VALID FOR UNLIMITED RENTRY

Visualize Your Success with Manifestation Props
VEHICLE TITLE

You now have a vehicle title for your: _____

Now give a detailed description of why you've received this title:

_____
_____
_____
_____
_____
_____
_____

STATE OF _____

CERTIFICATE OF TITLE FOR A VEHICLE

TITLE NO._____ DATE ISSUED:_____

VEHICLE ID NO.

VEHICLE PHOTO:

YR. MODEL:
MAKE:
MODEL:
BODY TYPE:

OTHER VEHICLE DETAILS:

OWNER NAME:

SIGNATURE: _____

Visualize Your Success with Manifestation Props
CERTIFICATE OF ACHIEVEMENT

You have just received a certificate of achievement for: _____
_____

Now give a detailed description of why you've received this honor:
_____
_____
_____
_____
_____
_____
_____

CERTIFICATE
of ACHIEVEMENT

This certificate is presented to

_____
(fill in your name above)

For outstanding achievement in the area of:

_____   _____
DATE   SIGNATURE

BEST AWARD

Visualize Your Success with Manifestation Props
VIP PASSES

You've just received all access passes for: _____

Now give a detailed description of why you've received these exclusive passes:

_____
_____
_____
_____
_____
_____

VIP — ALL ACCESS PASS
DETAILS:

VIP — ALL ACCESS PASS
DETAILS:

Visualize Your Success with # Manifestation Props
CERTIFICATE OF BIRTH

You now have a certificate of birth for: _____
_____
Now give a detailed description of how you've lovingly welcomed your bundle of joy:
_____
_____
_____
_____
_____
_____
_____

THE BEST HOSPITAL
CERTIFICATE OF BIRTH

This Certifies that _____

after an easy birth process, a healthy happy baby with

weight _____ lbs. _____ oz. was born in this Hospital

on the _____ day of _____

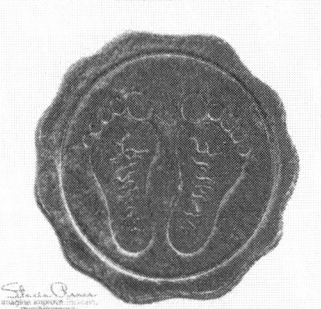

In Witness Whereof this Certificate has been duly signed by the Happy Parents.

_____
PARENTS

Visualize Your Success with Manifestation Props

BANK STATEMENT

Fill in your Bank Statement below. Then imagine and describe how you've been experiencing increase and financial abundance lately:

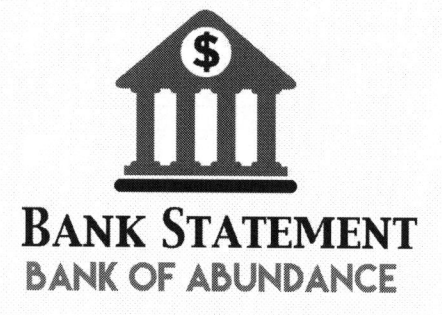

_____
_____
_____
_____

BANK STATEMENT
BANK OF ABUNDANCE

Account Number: _____
Statement Date:
Period Covered:

Name: _____
Address:

<Branch Name>

STATEMENT OF ACCOUNT

Page 1 of 1

Opening Balance:
Total Credit Amount:

Closing Balance:
Account Type:
Number of Transactions:

Transactions

Date	Description	Credit /Deposits	Balance

Visualize Your Success with Manifestation Props

UNLIMITED RECEIPT

My UNLIMITED RECEIPT

STORE NAME: _____
STORE ADDRESS: _____
DATE:
TIME:

QTY DESCRIPTION   PRICE   TOTAL

TAXABLE
TOTAL

ABC-3455-EFG-235

THANK YOU

You're headed out for a full day of shopping and money is no object. Where did you go and what did you buy? List your purchases on the receipt. Describe your amazing day of shopping below.

_____
_____
_____
_____
_____
_____
_____
_____
_____
_____
_____
_____
_____
_____
_____
_____
_____
_____
_____
_____
_____
_____
_____

Visualize Your Success with Manifestation Props
BLANK CHECKS

Write these blank checks to yourself with your current goal income amounts. Keep them here to view during your meditation time or cut them out and post them to view daily.

Unlimited Money Manifestation Bank
777 Believe it & Receive it Avenue
Everywhere, I AM

1111

DATE _____

$ _____

PAY TO THE ORDER OF _____ DOLLARS

This is a visualization tool from Dr. Stacia and Ariana Pierce

BANK OF WEALTH FOR ME
This is not an instrument subject to Article # of the UCC

FOR _____ Signed: _____

⑈00000 4444⑈ 000000529⑈ 1111   *imagine, improve, increase*   www.lifecoach2women.com

---

Unlimited Money Manifestation Bank
777 Believe it & Receive it Avenue
Everywhere, I AM

1111

DATE _____

$ _____

PAY TO THE ORDER OF _____ DOLLARS

This is a visualization tool from Dr. Stacia and Ariana Pierce

BANK OF WEALTH FOR ME
This is not an instrument subject to Article # of the UCC

FOR _____ Signed: _____

⑈00000 4444⑈ 000000529⑈ 1111   *imagine, improve, increase*   www.lifecoach2women.com

---

Unlimited Money Manifestation Bank
777 Believe it & Receive it Avenue
Everywhere, I AM

1111

DATE _____

$ _____

PAY TO THE ORDER OF _____ DOLLARS

This is a visualization tool from Dr. Stacia and Ariana Pierce

BANK OF WEALTH FOR ME
This is not an instrument subject to Article # of the UCC

FOR _____ Signed: _____

⑈00000 4444⑈ 000000529⑈ 1111   *imagine, improve, increase*   www.lifecoach2women.com

Visualize Your Success with Manifestation Props
BLANK CHECKS

Write these blank checks to yourself with your current goal income amounts. Keep them here to view during your meditation time or cut them out and post them to view daily.

Unlimited Money Manifestation Bank
777 Believe it & Receive it Avenue
Everywhere, I AM

1111

DATE _____

$ _____

PAY TO THE ORDER OF _____

DOLLARS

This is a visualization tool from Dr. Stacia and Ariana Pierce

BANK OF WEALTH FOR ME
This is not an instrument subject to Article # of the UCC

FOR _____   Signed: _____

⑈00000 4444⑈ 000000529⑈ 1111   www.lifecoach2women.com

Unlimited Money Manifestation Bank
777 Believe it & Receive it Avenue
Everywhere, I AM

1111

DATE _____

$ _____

PAY TO THE ORDER OF _____

DOLLARS

This is a visualization tool from Dr. Stacia and Ariana Pierce

BANK OF WEALTH FOR ME
This is not an instrument subject to Article # of the UCC

FOR _____   Signed: _____

⑈00000 4444⑈ 000000529⑈ 1111   www.lifecoach2women.com

Unlimited Money Manifestation Bank
777 Believe it & Receive it Avenue
Everywhere, I AM

1111

DATE _____

$ _____

PAY TO THE ORDER OF _____

DOLLARS

This is a visualization tool from Dr. Stacia and Ariana Pierce

BANK OF WEALTH FOR ME
This is not an instrument subject to Article # of the UCC

FOR _____   Signed: _____

⑈00000 4444⑈ 000000529⑈ 1111   www.lifecoach2women.com

Made in the USA
Columbia, SC
24 September 2023